A Beginning Look at
CANADA

THIRD EDITION

Anne-Marie Kaskens

PEARSON
Longman

5757 CYPIHOT STREET, SAINT-LAURENT (QUÉBEC) CANADA H4S 1R3
TELEPHONE: 1 800 263-3678 EXT. 232   FAX: 1 866 334-0448
infoesl@erpi.com   www.longman-esl.ca

Project editor
Linda Barton

Art director
Hélène Cousineau

Graphic design coordinator
Karole Bourgon

Cover design
Benoît Pitre

Page design and layout
Talisman illustration design

Photo Credits
Cover and title page photos: SHUTTERSTOCK (from left to right) Y. Arcurs / T. Olson / A. Pidjass / J. Zhou / J. Stitt; page 15, Report Terre / Gamma / PONOPRESSE; page 30, Dorling Kindersley; page 40, Dorling Kindersley; page 61, M. Ponomareff / PONOPRESSE; page 64, Royal Canadian Mint; page 78, Dorling Kindersley; page 79, Dorling Kindersley; page 79, Dorling Kindersley; page 82, Dorling Kindersley; page 90, Dorling Kindersley; page 92, Canadian Press NATARK; page 94, Dorling Kindersley; page 96, National Archives; page 98, Canadian Press CP; page 100, Ian Jones / Gamma / PONOPRESSE; page 100, Canada Post Corporation; page 100, Royal Canadian Mint; page 102, Canadian Press CP; page 104, Simon Grosset / Gamma / PONOPRESSE; page 108, Courtesy of Elections Canada; page 110, Canada Site, Communications Canada; page 112, Royal Canadian Mint; page 114, Courtesy of Elections Canada; page 114, Getstock / The Toronto Star; page 117, Courtesy of Elections Canada; page 124, Canadian Press CP; page 128, Canadian Press CP; page 130, Royal Canadian Mint; page 138, Canadian Press CP; page 141, Canadian Press CP; page 143, Canadian Press CP; page 148, Canadian Press CP; page 151, Royal Canadian Mint; page 156, Canadian Press CP; page 158, Canadian Press CP; page 164, Dorling Kindersley; page 164, Canadian Press CP.

© 2010 PEARSON Longman Published and distributed by
ÉDITIONS DU RENOUVEAU PÉDAGOGIQUE INC.

Registration of copyright: 3rd quarter 2010
Bibliothèque nationale du Québec
National Library of Canada
Printed in Canada

ISBN 978-2-7613-3551-5

234567890 IG 14 13 12
133551 ABCD   OF 10

TABLE OF CONTENTS

Preface	VI

PART 1–THE LAND
Canada's Provinces and Territories

Get Ready to Learn		2
Unit 1	The Size of Canada	3
Unit 2	The Provinces and Territories	5
Unit 3	The Capital Cities	12
Unit 4	Driving Across Canada	14
Unit 5	The Weather in Canada	15

Canada's Land

Get Ready to Learn		18
Unit 6	Canada's Land	19
Unit 7	The Forest	21
Unit 8	Canada's Water	22
Unit 9	Rock	24
Unit 10	Soil	26

Canada's Regions

Get Ready to Learn		27
Unit 11	Canada's Regions	28
Unit 12	The West Coast	30
Unit 13	The Prairie Provinces	33
Unit 14	Central Canada	35
Unit 15	The Atlantic Region	38
Unit 16	The North	40
Unit 17	Region Review	42
Glossary		43

PART 2–THE PEOPLE
Canada's Population

Get Ready to Learn		46
Unit 1	The World's Most Populated Countries	47
Unit 2	Population of Canada	49
Unit 3	Ages of Canadians	51
Unit 4	Populations of Canada's Provinces and Territories	53
Unit 5	Where Do Canadians Live?	55

Unit 6	Who Are Canadians?	56
Unit 7	Immigrants to Canada	58
Unit 8	Languages Canadians Speak	61

Canadians and Work

Get Ready to Learn		**63**
Unit 9	Canada's Currency	64
Unit 10	Canadians and Job Industries	67
Unit 11	The Minimum Wage	69
Unit 12	Earnings and Deductions	72
Unit 13	Unemployment	74
Glossary		**76**

PART 3–THE HISTORY
Canada's History

Get Ready to Learn		**78**
Unit 1	Aboriginal Peoples	79
Unit 2	New France	82
Unit 3	British Rule	84
Unit 4	Confederation	87
Unit 5	Aboriginal Peoples and European Settlement	90
Unit 6	Settling the West	92
Unit 7	Canada and the World Wars	94
Unit 8	The Constitution Act	96
Unit 9	The Canadian Charter of Rights and Freedoms	98
Unit 10	Celebrating Our History: Victoria Day	100
Unit 11	Celebrating Our History: Canada Day	102
Unit 12	Celebrating Our History: Aboriginal Peoples	104
Glossary		**105**

PART 4–THE GOVERNMENT
Canada's Government

Get Ready to Learn		**108**
Unit 1	The Levels of Government	109
Unit 2	Government Spending	112
Unit 3	Canada Is a Democracy	114
Unit 4	Who Can Vote?	117

The Federal Government

Unit 5	Ridings	120
Unit 6	Political Parties	124
Unit 7	Members of Parliament	126
Unit 8	House of Commons	128
Unit 9	Government Spending	130
Unit 10	The Prime Minister	132
Unit 11	Prime Ministers of Canada	136
Unit 12	The Cabinet	138
Unit 13	The Senate	141
Unit 14	The Governor General	143
Unit 15	Summary	145

The Provincial Government

Unit 16	Ridings	146
Unit 17	Members of Provincial Legislature	148
Unit 18	Government Spending	151
Unit 19	Political Parties	152
Unit 20	The Premier	153
Unit 21	The Cabinet	156
Unit 22	The Lieutenant Governor	158
Unit 23	Provincial Government: Summary	160
Unit 24	Provincial and Federal Government: Summary	161

The Municipal Government

Unit 25	The Municipal Government	162
Unit 26	Responsibilities	164
Unit 27	Members of Government	166
Unit 28	The Federal, Provincial and Municipal Government: Review	168
Glossary		172
Full Glossary		174

Preface

Many learners lack basic knowledge about Canadian geography, history and the workings of the Canadian government. Others lack this basic knowledge, and are also beginning learners of the English language. For these learners, reading texts that assume a background knowledge of Canada or a high level of English language competence can be frustrating and intimidating.

This book introduces students to essential facts about Canada in a clear language format. It provides an introductory overview of Canada's geography, people, history and government.

The text is designed for students (elementary, high school or adult) who want to learn about Canada. It is particularly useful to learners of English as a second language who also want to learn about Canada.

Organization of the Book

A Beginning Look at Canada is divided into four parts: **The Land**, **The People**, **The History** and **The Government**. Each part includes a number of short units, two to four pages in length. Each unit begins with information readings about an aspect of Canada and is followed by comprehension exercises.

Pre-Reading and Glossary

Each of the four parts begin with a page of questions titled **Get Ready to Learn**. These questions help to stimulate interest and trigger prior knowledge about the content of the part before it is read.

Each part ends with a glossary, in which key vocabulary words are defined.

Information Readings

There are seventy one-page information readings, each followed by comprehension exercises. The readings present information about Canada in a sequential, easy-to-understand format. The sentences are short, and the text does not assume background knowledge of Canada. Unit headings, subheadings, maps, pictures and charts are included to help the learner make sense of the text.

Comprehension Exercises

Each one-page information reading is followed by comprehension exercises. The exercises focus on the content of the reading and prompt the learner to re-read for details, to interpret charts and maps, to recall key facts and to define key vocabulary. It is the intention that learners "overlearn" some basic concepts about Canada, so they can build and retain a vocabulary and background knowledge about Canada.

A number of different exercises appear throughout the text. These include matching words to word meanings, multiple choice questions, filling in the blanks, correcting false sentences, sequencing events, crossword puzzles and discussion questions. Learners can complete the exercises individually, in pairs or in small groups.

The Teacher's Manual

The Teacher's Manual includes answer keys, pre-reading suggestions for each unit, reproducible classroom activities, and masters for making flashcards. The Teacher's Manual is available online.

Acknowledgements

I would like to thank the many literacy and ESL learners I have encountered who have taught me so much about learning. I would also like to thank Joy Lehmann, whose encouragement and trust helped me gain the confidence to write learning resources. Thank you also to Linda Barton (project editor) and Julie Hough (ERPI Vice-President, ESL).

PART 1
THE LAND

Canada's Provinces and Territories

Get Ready to Learn		**2**
Unit 1	The Size of Canada	**3**
Unit 2	The Provinces and Territories	**5**
Unit 3	The Capital Cities	**12**
Unit 4	Driving Across Canada	**14**
Unit 5	The Weather in Canada	**15**

Canada's Land

Get Ready to Learn		**18**
Unit 6	Canada's Land	**19**
Unit 7	The Forest	**21**
Unit 8	Canada's Water	**22**
Unit 9	Rock	**24**
Unit 10	Soil	**26**

Canada's Regions

Get Ready to Learn		**27**
Unit 11	Canada's Regions	**28**
Unit 12	The West Coast	**30**
Unit 13	The Prairie Provinces	**33**
Unit 14	Central Canada	**35**
Unit 15	The Atlantic Region	**38**
Unit 16	The North	**40**
Unit 17	Region Review	**42**

Glossary	**43**

TO LEARN ABOUT...
Canada's Provinces and Territories

In Units one to five, you will learn about Canada's provinces and territories.

Canada

Before you work on the units, try to answer these questions.

1. Do you think Canada is a big country compared with other countries in the world?
2. Is Canada larger than your country of origin?
3. About how many kilometres wide do you think Canada is, from east to west?
4. What continent is Canada in?
5. What continent is your country of origin in?
6. Can you name the provinces and territories of Canada?
7. Which provinces are next to an ocean?
8. What do you think happens in a capital city?
9. Can you name the capital city of Canada?
10. Can you name the capital city of the province you live in?
11. What is the capital city of your country of origin?
12. Describe the weather in Canada.
13. Describe the weather in your country of origin.

UNIT 1
THE SIZE OF CANADA

Canada is the second-largest country in the world. It is about 4,600 kilometres from north to south, and about 5,500 kilometres from east to west.

The Six Largest Countries

The six largest countries in the world are listed on the map. The United States is the fourth-largest country. Brazil is the fifth-largest, and Australia is the sixth-largest country in the world.

Where Is Canada?

Canada is in the continent of North America. North America includes Canada, the United States and Mexico.

A continent is a large area of land. There are seven continents in the world: North America, South America, Europe, Asia, Africa, Australia and Antarctica.

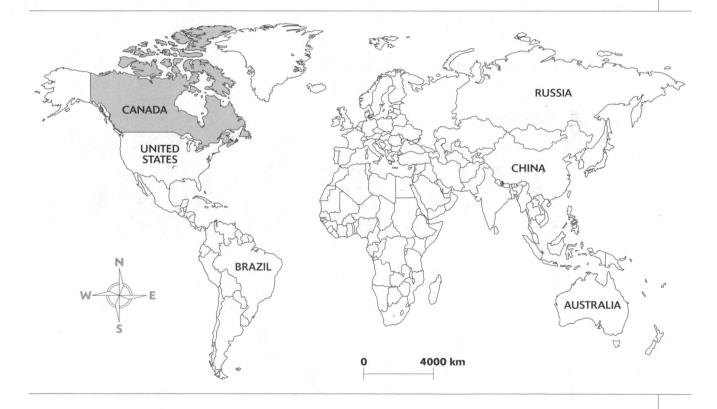

Understand What You Read

(A) **Answer the Questions**

1. Write the names of the countries on the lines.

Countries by Size
Largest   R
Second-largest   C
Third-largest   C
Fourth-largest   A
Fifth-largest   B
Sixth-largest   A

2. What is a continent?

3. How many continents are there in the world?

7

4. What continent is Canada in?

5. Name three countries in North America.

6. How long is Canada from north to south?

7. How wide is Canada from east to west?

(B) **Circle True or False**

1. Canada is the largest country in the world.   T   (F)

2. Canada is a large country.   (T)   F

3. Russia is larger than Canada.   (T)   F

4. The United States is larger than Canada.   T   (F)

Canada

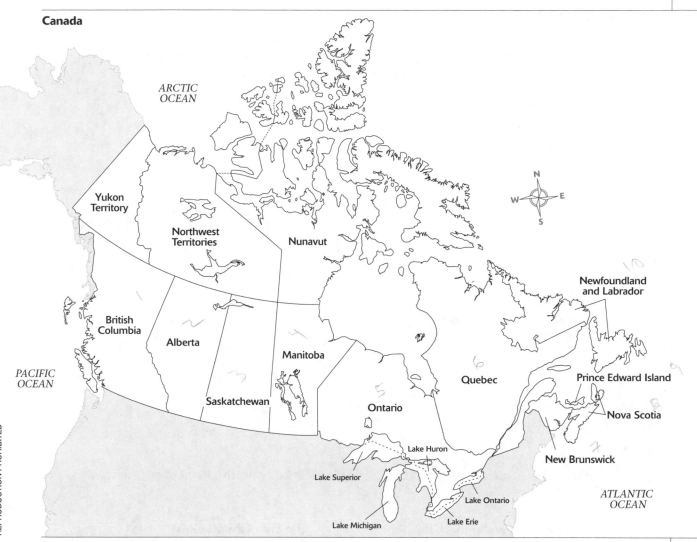

Provinces and Territories

There are ten provinces and three territories in Canada. The territories (Yukon Territory, Northwest Territories and Nunavut) are in the north of Canada.

Oceans

Three oceans surround Canada. The Atlantic Ocean is east of Canada. The Pacific Ocean is west of Canada. The Arctic Ocean is north of Canada.

Understand What You Read

A **Fill in the Blanks**

Look at the map on page 5.

Write the names of Canada's ten provinces and three territories on the lines.

Write the names as they appear on the map from west to east.

Canada's Ten Provinces
(from west to east)

British Columbia

_____   _____

_____   _____

_____   _____

_____   _____

Canada's Three Territories
(from west to east)

_____

_____

_____

Write the names of the oceans surrounding Canada and the five Great Lakes on the lines.

Oceans Surrounding Canada
(in any order)

_____

_____

_____

The Five Great Lakes
(between Ontario and the United States)

_____

_____

_____

_____

_____

B Fill in the Blanks

Write the provinces and territories on the map. Prince Edward Island is done for you.

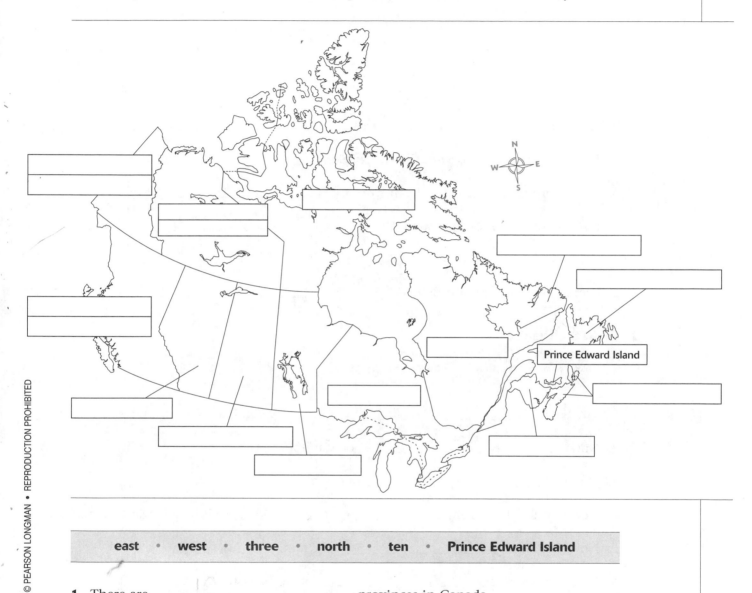

Prince Edward Island

---

east • west • three • north • ten • Prince Edward Island

1. There are _____ provinces in Canada.

2. There are _____ territories in Canada.

3. The smallest province is _____.

4. Canada's territories are in the _____ of Canada.

5. Nova Scotia is on the _____ side of Canada.

6. British Columbia is on the _____ side of Canada.

(C) Answer the Questions

1. List four provinces on the Atlantic Ocean.

_____

_____

_____

_____

2. Name one province on the Pacific Ocean.

_____

3. Which province is closest to the Great Lakes? _____

4. Which province is the smallest in size? _____

5. List two territories on the Arctic Ocean.

_____

_____

6. Name Canada's largest province.

_____

(D) Fill in the Blanks

north • south • east • west

1. The Yukon is _____ of British Columbia.

2. Nunavut is _____ of Manitoba.

3. Ontario is _____ of Quebec.

4. Newfoundland and Labrador is _____ of Prince Edward Island.

5. Nova Scotia is _____ of Ontario.

6. New Brunswick is _____ of Nova Scotia.

7. British Columbia is _____ of the Yukon.

8. Saskatchewan is _____ of Manitoba.

9. British Columbia is _____ of Saskatchewan.

E Complete the Crossword

Canada Post uses two-letter abbreviations for the provinces and territories. Write the full name of the correct province or territory beside each abbreviation. Then complete the crossword.

DOWN ↓	ACROSS →
1. NB _____	8. QC _____
2. MB _____	9. AB _____
3. NS _____	10. NU _____
4. PE _____	11. NT _____
5. BC _____	12. ON _____
6. YT _____	13. SK _____
7. NL _____	

F Match

Draw a line to match each map with the name of its province or territory.

Manitoba

Newfoundland and Labrador

Yukon Territory

Ontario

British Columbia

New Brunswick

Northwest Territories

Alberta

Prince Edward Island

Quebec

Nova Scotia

Nunavut

Saskatchewan

Capital Cities

Canada has a capital city. Each province and territory in Canada has a capital city, too.

The Capital City of Canada

The capital city of Canada is Ottawa. The federal government has its government offices there, in the **Parliament Buildings**. Federal politicians work in the Parliament Buildings.

Provincial and Territorial Capital Cities

The provinces and territories have capital cities, too. Each province has provincial government buildings in its capital city. Each territory has territorial government buildings in its capital city.

Understand What You Read

A **Fill in the Blanks**

Write each capital city beside its province or territory.

| Yellowknife • Regina • Victoria • Toronto • Charlottetown |
| St. John's • Winnipeg • Edmonton • Halifax |
| Whitehorse • Fredericton • Quebec City • Iqaluit |

Province or Territory	Capital City
British Columbia	
Alberta	
Saskatchewan	
Manitoba	
Ontario	
Quebec	
Newfoundland and Labrador	
New Brunswick	
Nova Scotia	
Prince Edward Island	
Yukon Territory	
Northwest Territories	
Nunavut	

B **Answer the Questions**

1. What is the capital city of Canada? _____

2. Which province is the capital city of Canada in? _____

3. What is the capital city of your province or territory? _____

4. How many capital cities are in Canada, including Ottawa? _____

5. What is the capital city of Ontario? _____

DRIVING ACROSS CANADA

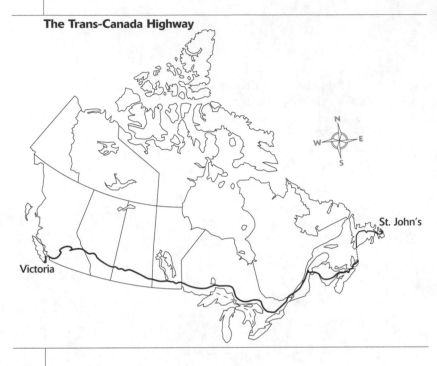

The Trans-Canada Highway

The Trans-Canada Highway

A highway crosses Canada from the east to the west. It is called the Trans-Canada Highway.

The Trans-Canada Highway is the longest highway in the world (that stays in one country). From St. John's in Newfoundland and Labrador to Victoria in British Columbia, the highway is 7,821 kilometres long.

Understand What You Read

(A) Answer the Questions

1. At 100 km an hour, about how many hours would it take to drive across Canada?

   _____

2. At 5 km an hour, about how many days would it take to walk across Canada?

   _____

3. These sentences are false. Change the underlined word to write a correct sentence on each line.

   a) A highway crosses Canada from <u>north to south</u>.

   _____

   b) It is called the <u>Trans-Ontario</u> Highway.

   _____

   c) It is the <u>widest</u> highway in the world.

   _____

   d) It is <u>8,721</u> kilometres long.

   _____

THE WEATHER IN CANADA

The weather varies in different parts of Canada. The North is the coldest part of Canada. The summers are short and the winters are long and very cold.

British Columbia is the most temperate province in Canada. **Temperate** means not too cold and not too hot. The winters there are milder than in other parts of Canada. The summers are warm but not too humid.

Many Canadians live in the southern part of Ontario. In this area, the summers are hot and more humid than in other parts of Canada.

The maps show how cold Canada gets in the winter, and how hot it gets in the summer in the capital cities.

WINTER - Average Low Temperature in Celsius for the Coldest Month

Whitehorse -22
Yellowknife -31
Edmonton -19
Regina -22
Victoria 1
Winnipeg -23
Quebec City -18
Toronto -10
Fredericton -15
Halifax -11
Charlottetown -13
St. John's -9

SUMMER - Average High Temperature in Celsius for the Warmest Month

Whitehorse 20
Yellowknife 21
Edmonton 22
Regina 26
Victoria 22
Winnipeg 26
Quebec City 25
Toronto 27
Fredericton 26
Halifax 24
Charlottetown 23
St. John's 20

Source: Adapted from the Statistics Canada website, Jan. 2010, http://www40.statcan.gc.ca/101/cst01/phys08b-eng.htm.

Understand What You Read

(A) Map Work

Look at the winter and summer maps on page 15. Fill in the names of the provinces or territories and write the average temperatures on the chart below.

Average Daily Temperature in Celsius for the Coldest and Warmest Months			
Province or Territory	Capital City	Average Low in Winter	Average High in Summer
British Columbia	Victoria	1	22
Alberta	Edmonton		
	Regina		
	Winnipeg		
	Toronto		
	Quebec City		
	Fredericton		
	Halifax		
	Charlottetown		
	St. John's		
	Whitehorse		
	Yellowknife		
	Iqaluit	data not available	

(B) Answer the Questions *(not including Iqaluit)*

1. Which capital city is the coldest in winter?

   _____

2. Which capital city is the warmest in winter?

   _____

3. Which capital city is the warmest in summer?

   _____

4. Which two capital cities are the coolest in the summer?

   _____

C) Map Work

Write the names of the provinces, territories and capital cities from warmest to coldest in the winter. Write the average low temperature beside each city.

Province or Territory	Capital City	WINTER Average Low Temperature

warmest in winter

coldest in winter

D) Match

Draw a line to match each word with its meaning.

Temperate	Moist
Humid	A unit of measurement in the metric system
Celsius	Mild

TO LEARN ABOUT...

Canada's Land

In Units six to ten, you will learn about Canada's land.

Before you work on the units, try to answer these questions.

1. Do you think Canada has many forests?

   Do you think Canada is   a) completely covered in forest?
                                 b) about half covered in forest?
                                 c) about a quarter covered in forest?

2. What do you think Canada produces from its forests?

3. Do you think Canada's soil is good for farming? What areas of Canada do you think are farmed?

4. Much of Canada is made up of tree-covered rock called the Canadian Shield. Which provinces or territories do you think contain the Canadian Shield? How do you think it can be used?

5. Look at a map of Canada in an atlas. List three oceans around Canada. List some of the large lakes of Canada.

6. There are mountains in parts of Canada. Which provinces or territories do you think have mountains?

CANADA'S LAND

Forest

Canada is a huge country, about half covered in forest. There are forests in every part of Canada except the far north. It is too cold for trees there.

Rock

A huge area of rock covers much of Canada. It is called the Canadian Shield. The Canadian Shield is over three billion years old. It is mostly covered by a thin layer of soil and forest. The Canadian Shield is in most of Canada's provinces and territories.

Soil

Most of Canada's soil is not farmed. In many parts of Canada, the soil is not deep enough. In other parts, the summers are not long enough. But in parts of southern Canada, the soil is rich and healthy. Most of Canada's farms are in these southern areas of Canada.

Water

Canada has lots of water. There are about two million freshwater lakes, and many rivers. Canada also borders three oceans: the Atlantic Ocean, the Pacific Ocean and the Arctic Ocean. Hudson Bay is a huge body of water in the middle of Canada.

Mountains

In parts of Canada there are mountains. Canada's highest mountains are in the Yukon and in British Columbia. Smaller rounded mountains are in eastern Canada.

Understand What You Read

A Match

Parts of southern Canada have many	far north.
A large body of water in the middle of Canada is	forest.
A huge area of rock in Canada is called	farms.
About half of Canada is covered in	Hudson Bay.
It is too cold for trees in the	the Canadian Shield.

B Answer the Questions

1. Why is the far north of Canada the least covered in forest?

   _____

2. What is the Canadian Shield?

   _____

3. About how old is the Canadian Shield?

   _____

4. Describe the soil on top of the Canadian Shield.

   _____

5. Where are Canada's highest mountains?

   _____

6. Where are most of Canada's farms?

   _____

7. About how much of Canada is covered in forest?

   _____

8. Name the huge body of water in the middle of Canada.

   _____

9. About how many freshwater lakes are in Canada?

   _____

10. Where in Canada are there small rounded mountains?

   _____

C Discuss

1. Describe the land in your country of origin. Are there many forests, farms, freshwater lakes, mountains or oceans?

2. Where would you most like to live: near mountains, farms or water? Why?

About half of Canada is covered in forest. There is forest in every province and territory.

Forests are a valuable natural resource for Canada.

Some of Canada's forests are protected by law. People cannot cut down the trees in protected forests.

How Are the Forests Used?

In some forests, loggers cut down trees and cut them into logs. Companies buy the logs to make lumber, wood and pulp and paper products.

Forest Cover in Canada

Forest

Understand What You Read

(A) Answer the Questions

1. Look at the "forest cover" map. Which territory is the least covered in forest?

   _____

2. Which provinces or territories are almost completely covered in forest?

   _____

3. Paper products are made from trees. List as many paper products as you can.

   _____

4. List as many wood products as you can.

   _____

5. Do you think we should be concerned about losing Canada's forests? Why?

   _____

Lakes, Rivers and Oceans

Almost 10 percent of Canada is covered with freshwater lakes and rivers. There are about two million freshwater lakes in Canada, and many rivers. Canada also borders three oceans.

How Is Canada's Water Used?

Canada's water is a valuable natural resource. Canada uses its water for many things. We use water in homes and businesses, on farms and in factories. We also use water to transport products and people by boat, as a source of electricity and for catching fish.

Fishing

On the east and west coasts of Canada, many people fish in the coastal waters. Many others work in factories producing fish products. The fish catch and seafood production in Canada has been decreasing over the past fifty years. This is because of warmer temperatures and over-fishing. Canada wants to make sure we don't over-fish our waters. The government has rules about how many fish we can take from the ocean.

Hydroelectricity

The word **hydro** means water. Hydroelectricity is electricity that is made from moving water. About 60 percent of Canada's electricity is hydroelectricity. Canada also makes electricity from coal, oil and nuclear power. British Columbia and Quebec produce the most hydroelectricity in Canada.

Understand What You Read

(A) Discuss

1. There is a lot of water in Canada. Are there many lakes and rivers in your country of origin?

2. Salmon and crab are two common sea animals in Canada's coastal waters. Make a list of other common sea animals. Which sea animals do you like best?

3. Some Canadians work as fishers. Which provinces do you think these Canadians work in?

B **Answer the Questions**

1. List three oceans that border Canada.

_____

2. About how much of Canada is covered in freshwater lakes and rivers?

_____

3. About how many freshwater lakes are in Canada?

_____

4. List five uses for Canada's water.

_____

5. In which provinces do you think people have jobs as fishers?

_____

6. Why has the fish catch in Canada decreased over the past fifty years?

_____

7. What does **hydro** mean?

_____

8. What is hydroelectricity?

_____

9. Which provinces produce the most hydroelectricity?

_____

10. List three other sources of electricity.

_____

The Canadian Shield

Canadian Shield

About half of Canada is covered by a huge area of rock called the Canadian Shield.

The Canadian Shield is covered by a thin layer of soil and forest, with many small lakes and rivers.

Where Is the Canadian Shield?

The Canadian Shield covers about half of Canada's land. It is a large U-shaped area that surrounds Hudson Bay.

How Does Canada Use the Canadian Shield?

There are many minerals in the rock of the Canadian Shield. These minerals are a valuable resource. Some of the minerals in the Canadian Shield are copper, zinc, iron, gold, silver, nickel and coal. Coal is a black rock that is burned to make electricity.

There are mines in most of Canada's provinces and territories. Many of Canada's mines are in northern Ontario and Quebec. Miners extract minerals from the mines. The minerals are used to make many of the items we use every day, such as cars, tools, wire and appliances.

Canada's Sedimentary Rock

Canada has a lot of sedimentary rock, too. Sedimentary rock is different from the rock of the Canadian Shield.

What Is Sedimentary Rock?

Moving rivers carry sediment along with water. Sediment includes sand, mud, older rocks, and plant and animal life. Over time, layers and layers of sediment settle on the ground. After many years the sediment layers get hard and become sedimentary rock.

Sedimentary rock contains oil and natural gas. Oil and gas are valuable resources. They are used to produce gasoline, jet fuel, heat and electricity for homes and businesses.

Sedimentary rock is on the ocean floor in coastal areas of Canada. It is also in parts of Canada. Much of Canada's sedimentary rock is in Alberta and Saskatchewan, parts of the Atlantic provinces and in the western half of the Northwest Territories.

Most of Canada's oil and natural gas is found in Alberta.

Understand What You Read

(A) **Answer the Questions**

1. Look at the map of Canada on page 24. List the provinces and territories that contain parts of the Canadian Shield.

   _____

2. How does Canada use coal?

   _____

3. List five minerals found in the Canadian Shield.

   _____

4. Write **southeast** or **southwest** on the lines.

   a) The _____ corner of Ontario is not covered by the Canadian Shield.

   b) The _____ corner of Quebec is not covered by the Canadian Shield.

5. What is sediment?

   _____

6. Why is sedimentary rock a valuable resource?

   _____

7. In which province is most of Canada's oil and natural gas found?

   _____

8. What can we make from oil and gas?

   _____

9. Where is there sedimentary rock in Canada?

   _____

SOIL

The Soil in Canada

Not much of Canada's soil is farmed. In the far north, the soil is always frozen. In many parts of Canada, the growing season is too short for crop farming. On much of the Canadian Shield, the layer of soil on the rock is too thin.

In parts of southern Canada, the soil is very healthy. Most of Canada's farms are there.

There are about 230,000 farms in Canada.

Number of Farms in Canada, 2006		
Region	Province or Territory	Farms
Atlantic Region	Newfoundland & Labrador	558
	Prince Edward Island	1,700
	Nova Scotia	3,795
	New Brunswick	2,776
Central Canada	Quebec	30,675
	Ontario	57,211
Prairie Provinces	Manitoba	19,054
	Saskatchewan	44,329
	Alberta	49,431
The West Coast	British Columbia	19,844
The North	Yukon	148
	Northwest Territories	33
	Nunavut	0

Source: Adapted from the Statistics Canada website, Jan. 2010, http://www.statcan.gc.ca/pub/95-629-x/.

Canada's Farms

Canada's livestock farms include dairy and beef cattle, hogs, poultry, sheep and goats.

Canada's crop farms include wheat and other grains, barley, corn and potatoes.

Canada also produces fruit.

Understand What You Read

(A) Answer the Questions

1. Which region of Canada has the most farms?

   _____

2. Which region of Canada has the fewest farms?

   _____

3. About how many farms are there in Canada?

   _____

TO LEARN ABOUT...
Canada's Regions

In Units eleven to seventeen, you will learn about Canada's regions.

Before you work on the units, try to answer these questions.

Canada is divided into five regions: the North, the West Coast, the Prairie provinces, Central Canada and the Atlantic region.

1. The five regions are shaded on the maps below. Try to write the correct region under each map.

_____

_____

_____

_____

_____

2. Which region do you think is the most populated? _____

3. Which region do you think is the least populated? _____

4. Which regions have coastal areas? _____

CANADA'S REGIONS

Canada has five regions. The land in each region is different from the other regions.

The West Coast

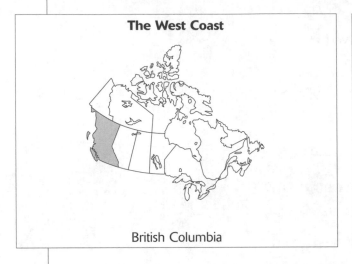

British Columbia

The Prairie Provinces

Alberta • Saskatchewan • Manitoba

Central Canada

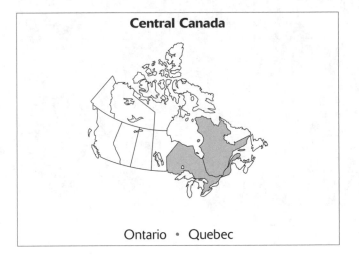

Ontario • Quebec

The Atlantic Region

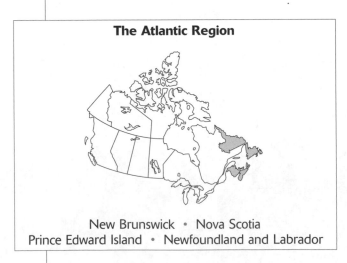

New Brunswick • Nova Scotia
Prince Edward Island • Newfoundland and Labrador

The North

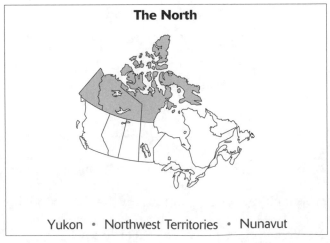

Yukon • Northwest Territories • Nunavut

Understand What You Read

(A) Fill in the Blanks

Shade the correct provinces or territories for each region. Write the correct provinces or territories under each region.

The Prairie Provinces

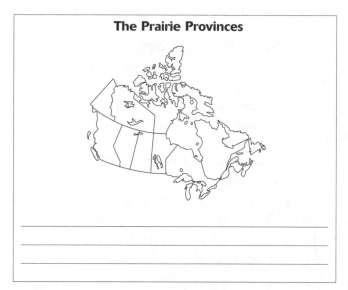

_____
_____
_____

The Atlantic Region

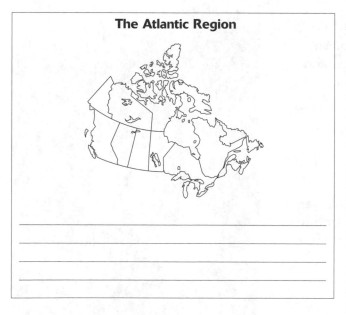

_____
_____
_____
_____

The West Coast

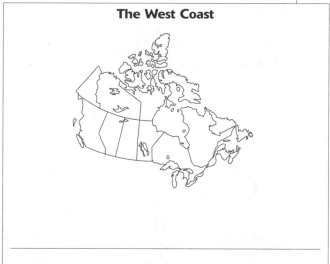

_____

Central Canada

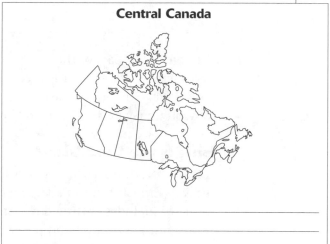

_____
_____

The North

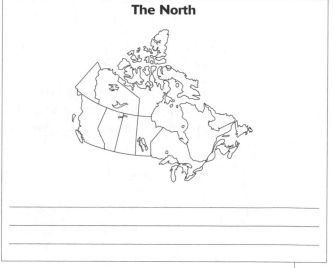

_____
_____
_____

The West Coast

Vancouver Island

British Columbia is the only province in the West Coast region.

Why Is It Called the West Coast?

British Columbia is the western-most province in Canada. It is also the only province that is next to the Pacific Ocean. Land next to the ocean is called **coast**.

What Does It Look Like?

Most of British Columbia is covered in forest and mountains. The **Rocky Mountains** of British Columbia are among the tallest in Canada.

Cities on the West Coast

Most people in British Columbia live in the southwest part of the province. Two large cities in British Columbia are Vancouver and Victoria. Vancouver is the largest city in British Columbia, and is Canada's third-largest city. Victoria is the capital city of British Columbia. It is on Vancouver Island. Vancouver Island is off British Columbia's southwest coast.

How Is the Land Used?

British Columbia has the most valuable forestry industry in Canada. The forestry industry includes cutting down trees and making lumber, wood and paper products.

Some of the land is used for farming. Cattle, fruit and horse farms are most common.

People fish for salmon and other fish off the coast of British Columbia.

British Columbia uses its fast-moving waters to make hydroelectric power. Most of British Columbia's electricity is generated from water.

Understand What You Read

© PEARSON LONGMAN • REPRODUCTION PROHIBITED

(A) **Answer the Questions**

1. How many provinces are on the West Coast?

   _____

2. Why is it called the West Coast?

   _____

3. Describe the land in British Columbia.

   _____

4. Victoria is on an island that belongs to British Columbia. Name the island.

   _____

5. Draw a line to match the resources with how they are used.

West Coast Resources	Using the Resources
forest	salmon fishing
soil	hydroelectric power
moving water	fruit and vegetables
ocean	wood and paper products

(B) **Correct the Sentences**

Each of the sentences is false. Circle the word that makes the sentence false. Then write a correct sentence on the line.

1. The West Coast is on the east side of Canada.

   _____

2. The West Coast is on the Atlantic Ocean.

   _____

3. The capital city of British Columbia is Vancouver.

   _____

4. Vancouver is Canada's largest city.

   _____

(C) Crossword

Try to complete the crossword without looking at the word list.

ACROSS →
1. Electricity made from water
2. Vancouver is our ____ largest city.
3. A province in the West Coast region
4. A product made from trees
5. Land that lies beside the ocean
6. The largest city in British Columbia
7. Land that is full of trees
8. An island of British Columbia
9. British Columbia is ____ of Alberta.

DOWN ↓
10. A product made from trees
11. Forest and ____ cover most of BC.
12. A mountain range in British Columbia
13. The capital of British Columbia
14. A kind of salt water fish
15. British Columbia is beside the ____ ocean.
16. Another word for the sea
17. There is ____ province on the West Coast.

Word List

| one • forest • lumber • Victoria • British Columbia |
| Rocky Mountains • coast • paper • salmon |
| Vancouver • Pacific • mountains • west • third • ocean |
| Vancouver Island • hydroelectricity |

THE PRAIRIE PROVINCES

There are three provinces in the Prairie provinces.

Why Is the Region Called the Prairie Provinces?

The word **prairie** means flat grassy land. The land in the southern part of the Prairie provinces is flat and grassy.

What Does It Look Like?

The northern half of this region is covered in forest.

The southern half is mostly flat with very rich soil. Many large farms cover the southern part of the Prairie provinces.

The Prairie Provinces

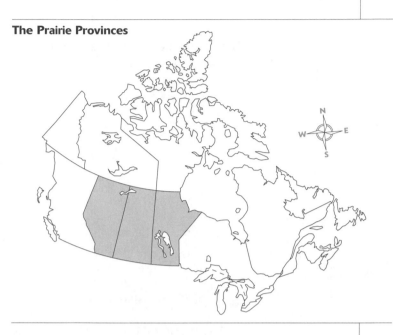

Cities in the Prairie Provinces

The five largest cities in the Prairie provinces are Calgary, Edmonton, Winnipeg, Saskatoon and Regina.

How Is the Land Used?

Most of the land in the southern half of the Prairie provinces is farmed. Most of the farms there are cattle, wheat and grain farms.

Wheat is used to make bread. For this reason, we sometimes call the Prairie provinces Canada's breadbasket.

Mining

There are large areas of sedimentary rock in the Prairie provinces. Oil and natural gas are mined from the rock. There are many oil and gas deposits in northern Alberta. Alberta makes most of Canada's oil and natural gas.

Understand What You Read

A) Match

Write the correct letter on the lines to match the words with their meanings.
The first one is done for you.

___c___ Capital of Alberta   a) Flat grassy land

_____ Canada's breadbasket   b) Alberta, Saskatchewan and Manitoba

_____ Three   c) Edmonton

_____ Prairie provinces   d) Winnipeg

_____ Covered in farms   e) Regina

_____ Prairie   f) Another name for the Prairie provinces

_____ Capital of Saskatchewan   g) Used to make bread

_____ Northern Alberta   h) Number of provinces in the Prairie provinces

_____ Capital of Manitoba   i) Southern half of the Prairie provinces

_____ Wheat   j) Has lots of oil and gas deposits

B) Map Work

Use a map of Canada to find Calgary, Edmonton, Regina, Saskatoon and Winnipeg.
Then write the correct letter (for each city) on the lines.

Most Populated Cities in the Prairie Province

Calgary   _____

Edmonton   _____

Regina   _____

Saskatoon   _____

Winnipeg   _____

Which three cities are capital cities?

_____

UNIT 14
CENTRAL CANADA

Central Canada

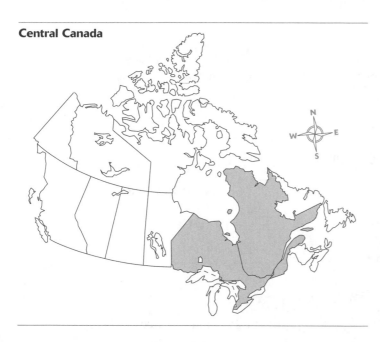

There are two provinces in Central Canada.

Why Is It Called Central Canada?

Central means near the centre. The provinces of Central Canada are the two largest, most populated provinces of Canada.

What Does It Look Like?

Most of Central Canada is covered by a large area of forest-covered rock called the Canadian Shield.

Central Canada is full of rivers and lakes. It has more freshwater than any other region in Canada. Ontario is home to the **Great Lakes**. There is a huge river in Quebec called the **St. Lawrence River**.

Cities in Central Canada

Most people in Central Canada live in cities in the south-central part of the region. The five largest cities there are Toronto, Montreal, Ottawa-Hull, Quebec City and Hamilton. Toronto and Montreal are the most populated cities in Canada.

How Is the Land Used?

Miners dig for minerals in the Canadian Shield. Companies use the minerals to make many of the products we use every day. The forest is used to make wood, pulp and paper products. We use some of the water in Central Canada to generate hydroelectricity.

The land in the south is used for farming. There are all kinds of farms in the southern part of Central Canada. The most common farms are cattle and grain farms.

Toronto

Understand What You Read

(A) Fill in the Blanks

| rock • forest • east • populated • freshwater |
| Quebec • Toronto • Ontario • minerals • paper |

1. The two provinces in Central Canada are _____ and _____.

2. _____ is the capital city of Ontario.

3. Central Canada is the most _____ region in Canada.

4. Central Canada has the most _____ in Canada.

5. The Canadian Shield is a large area of _____.

6. The Canadian Shield is covered in _____.

7. Central Canada is _____ of the Prairie provinces.

8. Miners dig for _____ in the Canadian Shield.

9. The forest is used to make wood, pulp and _____ products.

(B) Map Work

Use a map of Canada to find the Great Lakes and the St. Lawrence River. Then write the correct letter for each lake or river on the lines.

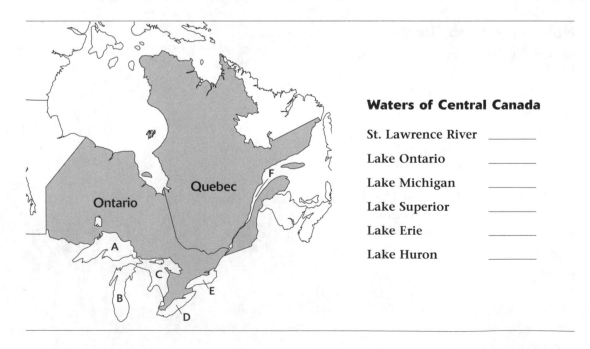

Waters of Central Canada

St. Lawrence River _____

Lake Ontario _____

Lake Michigan _____

Lake Superior _____

Lake Erie _____

Lake Huron _____

C) Crossword

Try to complete the crossword without looking at the word list.

ACROSS →

1. Central Canada is Canada's most ____ region.
2. The capital city of Quebec
3. On top of the Canadian Shield
4. There are ____ provinces in Central Canada.
5. There are ____ Great Lakes.
6. Copper, iron ore, nickel and silver are ____.
7. A province in Central Canada
8. Lake ____ is the only Great Lake that is entirely in the United States.
9. A Great Lake west of Lake Michigan

DOWN ↓

10. A large city in Ontario
11. A province in Central Canada
12. Ontario and Quebec
13. Five large lakes in Central Canada
14. A large area of rock covered with forest
15. A large city in Quebec
16. The capital city of Ontario
17. The capital city of Canada
18. The St. Lawrence is a large ____ in Quebec.

Word List

Ontario • Montreal • five • Hamilton • two • Superior
river • Central Canada • Ottawa • Great Lakes
Toronto • Michigan • forest • Quebec • Canadian Shield
minerals • Quebec City • populated

There are four provinces in the Atlantic region.

Why Is It Called the Atlantic Region?

The Atlantic region is next to the Atlantic Ocean. Sometimes we call the Atlantic region the **Maritimes** or the **East Coast**. A **coast** is land beside the ocean.

The Atlantic Region

What Does It Look Like?

There are farms, cities and towns and many small fishing villages in the Atlantic region.

The Provinces of the Atlantic Region

Newfoundland and Labrador is mostly rocky with many small lakes and rivers. Many fish live in the coastal waters.

Prince Edward Island is the smallest province in Canada. The soil is rich and healthy. Many farms are there.

New Brunswick and Nova Scotia are mostly covered in forest. There are also many farms.

How Is the Land Used?

Loggers cut down trees in some of the forests. Companies use the wood to make lumber, pulp and paper products.

People fish in the coastal waters of the Atlantic provinces. Lobster and crab are the most valuable seafood in the Atlantic region.

There are many farms in most of the Atlantic provinces. A lot of them are cattle farms. Farmers also grow fruit and potatoes.

Understand What You Read

(A) Map Work

Use a map of Canada to find the four provinces of the Atlantic region. Then write the correct letter for each province on the line.

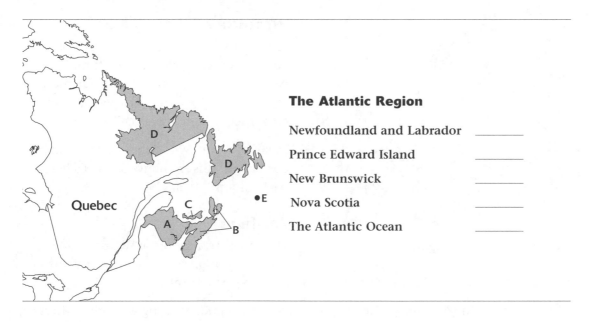

The Atlantic Region

Newfoundland and Labrador _____

Prince Edward Island _____

New Brunswick _____

Nova Scotia _____

The Atlantic Ocean _____

(B) Fill in the Blanks

Write the name of the correct Atlantic province on the line.

1. The smallest province in the Atlantic region is _____.

2. The province with the longest coastline in the Atlantic region is

_____.

3. The largest province in the Atlantic region is _____.

4. _____ is completely surrounded by water.

5. _____ and _____ border Quebec.

6. _____ is north of Prince Edward Island.

7. _____ is east of New Brunswick.

UNIT 16
THE NORTH

The North

There are three territories in the North. The winters are long and very cold in the North. The summers are short.

What Does It Look Like?

The North is the largest region in Canada, but it has the smallest population. It is partly covered in forest. In the far north, the land is frozen all year. Trees do not grow there. That land is called **tundra**.

Mountains and wilderness cover most of the **Yukon**. It is home to Canada's highest peak, Mount Logan.

The Inuit

The Inuit are a group of Aboriginal people. Aboriginal people were the first people to live in Canada. They have lived in Canada for thousands of years.

Most Inuit live in **Nunavut**. Some Inuit live by hunting and trapping animals. Others make soapstone carvings and other artwork. The art is sold all over Canada.

The Inuit have lived in Canada for thousands of years.

How Is the Land Used?

There are gold, lead and zinc mines in the North. There are also oil and gas deposits. Some people have jobs working in the mines or looking for other mineral and oil deposits.

Understand What You Read

(A) Answer the Questions

1. List the capital cities of each territory in the North.

   Yukon _____

   Northwest Territories _____

   Nunavut _____

2. Why are there no trees in the far north?

   _____

3. Name Canada's highest peak. Where is it?

   _____

4. Who are Aboriginal peoples?

   _____

5. Most Inuit live in which territory?

   _____

6. What types of mines are in the North?

   _____

7. Which territory has mountains?

   _____

8. Which territory is on the east side of Canada?

   _____

9. Which territory has many islands?

   _____

10. What is the weather like in the North?

   _____

(B) Discuss

1. Why do you think so few people live in the North?

| The North • The West Coast • The Prairie provinces |
| Central Canada • The Atlantic region |

Write the region that

1. Is mostly flat in the southern part _____

2. Has the highest mountain in Canada _____

3. Is on the Pacific Ocean _____

4. Is on the Atlantic Ocean _____

5. Is the largest in size _____

6. Is the most populated _____

7. Produces the most forestry products _____

8. Is sometimes called Canada's breadbasket _____

9. Is the least populated _____

10. Is the smallest in size _____

11. Has the most freshwater lakes and rivers _____

12. Has many fishing villages _____

13. Is mostly covered by the Canadian Shield _____

14. Produces the most oil and gas _____

15. Has territories _____

16. Is home to most of the Inuit _____

GLOSSARY
THE LAND

Atlantic region:	Nova Scotia, New Brunswick, Prince Edward Island and Newfoundland and Labrador
Canada:	The northernmost country in North America
Canada's breadbasket:	Another name for the Prairie provinces
Canadian Shield:	A large area of rock in Canada
Capital city:	The city in which the government is based
Celsius:	A unit of metric measurement used to measure temperature
Central Canada:	Ontario and Quebec
Coal:	A black mineral burned to make electricity
Coast:	Land beside the ocean
Continent:	A large area of land
East Coast:	Another name for the Atlantic region
Great Lakes:	Five large lakes in southern Ontario
Hudson Bay:	A large body of water in the middle of Canada
Humid:	Moist
Hydroelectricity:	Electricity made from moving water
Metric system:	A system for measuring distance, weight, mass and temperature
Mount Logan:	Canada's highest mountain
North (the):	Yukon Territory, the Northwest Territories and Nunavut
North America:	A continent that includes Canada, the United States and Mexico
Parliament Buildings:	The federal government buildings in Ottawa
Population:	The number of people who live in a place
Prairie provinces:	Manitoba, Saskatchewan and Alberta
Rocky Mountains:	Mountains in Western Canada
Sedimentary rock:	Rock made by rivers carrying sediment
Temperate:	Not too hot and not too cold
Trans-Canada Highway:	A highway that crosses southern Canada
Vancouver Island:	An island of British Columbia
Wheat:	A grain used to make bread

PART 2
THE PEOPLE

Canada's Population

Get Ready to Learn		**46**
Unit 1	The World's Most Populated Countries	**47**
Unit 2	Population of Canada	**49**
Unit 3	Ages of Canadians	**51**
Unit 4	Populations of Canada's Provinces and Territories	**53**
Unit 5	Where Do Canadians Live?	**55**
Unit 6	Who Are Canadians?	**56**
Unit 7	Immigrants to Canada	**58**
Unit 8	Languages Canadians Speak	**61**

Canadians and Work

Get Ready to Learn		**63**
Unit 9	Canada's Currency	**64**
Unit 10	Canadians and Job Industries	**67**
Unit 11	The Minimum Wage	**69**
Unit 12	Earnings and Deductions	**72**
Unit 13	Unemployment	**74**
Glossary		**76**

TO LEARN ABOUT...

Canada's Population

In Units one to eight, you will learn about Canada's population.

Before you work on the units, try to answer these questions.

1. Do you think Canada is a populated country compared with other countries in the world?

2. Which country do you think is the most populated country in the world?

3. Where in Canada do you think most Canadians live?

4. Which provinces do you think are the most populated in Canada? Why do you think these provinces are the most populated?

5. Which provinces or territories do you think are the least populated? Why do you think these provinces or territories are the least populated in Canada?

6. What do you think the most common language is in Canada, besides English and French?

7. About how many people do you think immigrate to Canada every year?

8. Where do you think many of these immigrants come from?

THE WORLD'S MOST POPULATED COUNTRIES

In land size, Canada is the second-biggest country in the world. But not many people live in Canada. Canada has a low population compared with many other countries. About 34 million people live in Canada (according to Statistics Canada's December 2009 population estimate).

There are about 6.8 billion people in the world.

10 Most Populated Countries	
1. China	1,331,000,000
2. India	1,171,000,000
3. United States	307,000,000
4. Indonesia	243,000,000
5. Brazil	191,000,000
6. Pakistan	181,000,000
7. Bangladesh	162,000,000
8. Nigeria	153,000,000
9. Russia	142,000,000
10. Japan	128,000,000

Source: Adapted from the 2009 World Population Data Sheet, Population Reference Bureau, Jan. 2010, http://www.prb.org/pdf09/09wpds_eng.pdf.

The Ten Most Populated Countries

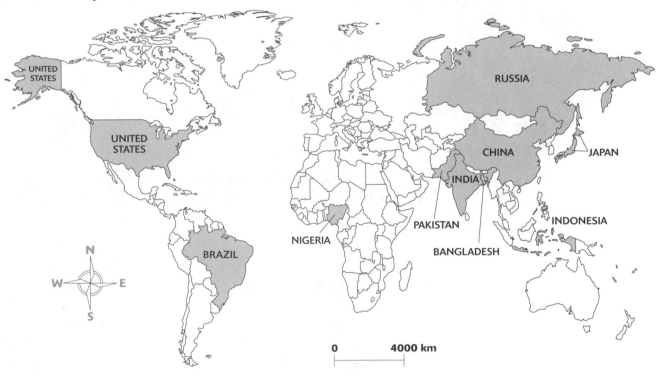

Understand What You Read

A) Answer the Questions

Look at the *"Most Populated Countries"* table and map on the previous page.

1. Which country has the highest population?_____

2. Which country is the largest in size?_____

3. Which country is closest to Canada?_____

4. Which country is the smallest in size?_____

5. Which two countries have a combined
   population of over two billion people?_____

6. Which country has the third-highest
   population? _____

7. What is the population of Canada?_____

8. What is the population of the world?_____

9. What is the population of your country
   of origin? _____

B) Match

Draw a line to match the word boxes with the number boxes.

one million = 1,000,000
one billion = 1,000 million = 1,000,000,000

The world's population	1,331 million
Canada's population	34 million
China's population	1,171 million
India's population	1,000 million
1 million	6.8 billion
1 billion	1,000,000

PART **TWO** - **THE PEOPLE**

UNIT 2
POPULATION OF CANADA

About 34 million people live in Canada today.

How Do We Know the Population of Canada?
Every five years the government counts the people who live in Canada. This count is called a **census**.

Canada Is Growing

In the 100 year period between 1901 and 2001, Canada's population grew from about 5 million people to about 30 million people.

From the 2006 census, we know that Canada's population is still growing (31,613,000 people), but that the rate of growth is slowing down. Women are giving birth to fewer children.

Each year, many people immigrate to Canada from other countries. This helps Canada's population grow.

Canada's Census Population Over 100 Years	
Year	Population
1901	5,371,000
1921	8,787,000
1941	11,507,000
1961	18,238,000
1981	24,343,000
2001	30,007,000

Source: Adapted from the Statistics Canada website, Jan. 2010, http://geodepot.statcan.ca/Diss/Highlights/Tables_e.pdf.

Understand What You Read

(A) Graph Work

Put a dot on the graph to show what Canada's population was in 1921, 1941, 1961, 1981 and 2001 (1901 is done for you). Then draw a line to connect the dots.

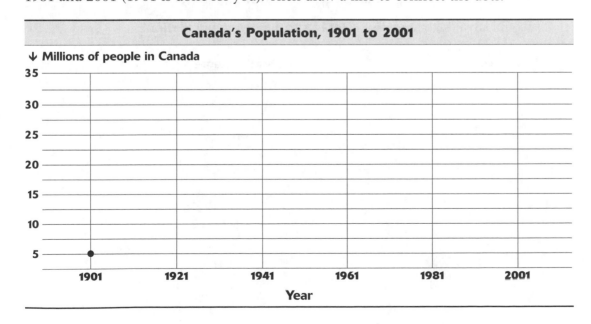

Canada's Population, 1901 to 2001

↓ Millions of people in Canada

B Answer the Questions

1. What is the population of Canada?

_____

2. What is a census?

_____

3. How often is there a census in Canada?

_____

4. There was a census in 2001 and 2006. When will the next census be taken?

_____

5. What was Canada's population in 1901?

_____

6. Why is Canada's population growth slowing down?

_____

7. List one reason why Canada's population is still growing.

_____

8. Look at the graph you drew on page 49. What does the graph show?

_____

C Discuss

1. Do you think Canada's population will keep growing? Why?

2. List some advantages and disadvantages to a growing population.

Advantages	Disadvantages

The number of Canadians in each age group is slowly changing. The number of Canadians who are under 45 is decreasing. The number of Canadians who are over 45 is increasing. People are living longer, people are healthier and women in Canada are having fewer babies.

Births in Canada

Canadian women are having fewer babies than they did in the past. They are also waiting until later in life to have children.

Canada's Seniors

About 14 percent of Canadians are seniors. Seniors are people who are 65 or older.

The number of seniors in Canada is growing. In 1921, only about 5 percent of Canadians were seniors. We predict that in 20 years, about 23 percent of our population will be made up of seniors.

Understand What You Read

 Discuss

1. Why do you think many women wait until they are older to have children?

2. Why do you think Canadian women are having fewer children?

3. A growing senior population will change some features of life in Canada. What things do you think will change? Make a list.

B Fill in the Blanks

1. The number of Canadians in each age group is _____.

2. People are living _____.

3. Women are having _____ babies.

4. Women are waiting until _____ in life to have children.

5. The number of Canadian _____ is growing.

6. A senior is a person aged 65 or _____.

C Answer the Questions

Number of Canadians in Age Groups *(Rounded)*			
Age Group	1981 (millions)	2006 (millions)	2031 Prediction (millions)
0 – 24	10.14	9.80	8.26
25 – 44	7.18	8.83	9.38
45 – 64	4.66	8.65	9.56
65 and over	2.36	4.34	8.86
TOTAL	24.34	31.62	36.06

Source: Adapted from Statistics Canada websites, Jan. 2010, http://www12.statcan.gc.ca/censusrecensement/2006/ (1981, 2006) and http://www40.statcan.gc.ca/cbin/fl/cstprintflag.cgi (2031 estimates).

1. In 1981, which age group was the largest?

_____

2. In 2031, which age group is predicted to be the largest?

_____

3. Between 1981 and 2006, which age groups increased the most in numbers?

_____

4. Between 2006 and 2031, which age group is predicted to increase the most in numbers?

_____

POPULATIONS OF CANADA'S PROVINCES AND TERRITORIES

The population numbers for each Canadian province and territory are listed below. Use the hints to write the correct population numbers on the map. Some are done for you.

Check your answers on the next page.

Hints

1. Ontario is the most populated province in Canada.
2. The three territories are the least populated areas in Canada.
3. The Yukon has a lower population than the Northwest Territories.
4. The Atlantic provinces are the least populated provinces of Canada.
5. Prince Edward Island is the least populated province in Canada.
6. Nova Scotia is more populated than New Brunswick.
7. British Columbia is the third most populated province of Canada.
8. Quebec is more populated than British Columbia.
9. Alberta is more populated than Manitoba.

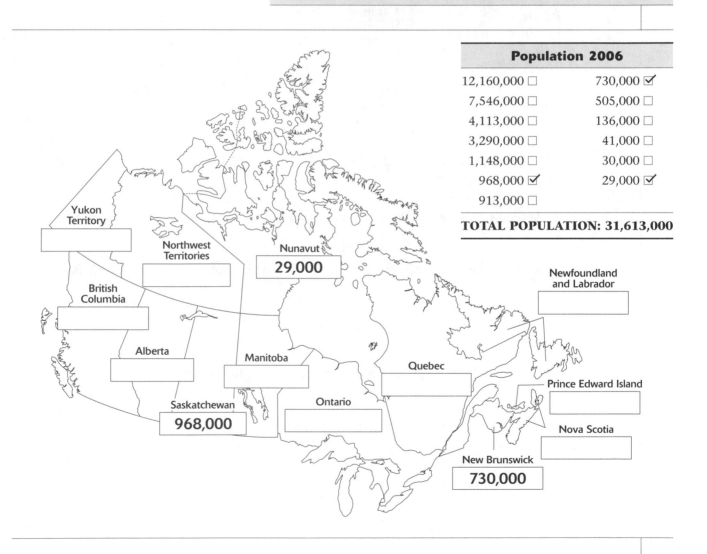

Population 2006

12,160,000 ☐	730,000 ☑
7,546,000 ☐	505,000 ☐
4,113,000 ☐	136,000 ☐
3,290,000 ☐	41,000 ☐
1,148,000 ☐	30,000 ☐
968,000 ☑	29,000 ☑
913,000 ☐	

TOTAL POPULATION: 31,613,000

Yukon Territory

Northwest Territories

Nunavut
29,000

Newfoundland and Labrador

British Columbia

Alberta

Manitoba

Quebec

Prince Edward Island

Saskatchewan
968,000

Ontario

Nova Scotia

New Brunswick
730,000

Understand What You Read

(A) **Answer the Questions**

Look at the chart below. Answer the questions that follow.

Population: Canada's Provinces and Territories 2001 and 2006			
Region	**Province or Territory**	**2001**	**2006**
Atlantic Region	Newfoundland & Labrador	513,000	505,000
	Prince Edward Island	135,000	136,000
	Nova Scotia	908,000	913,000
	New Brunswick	729,000	730,000
Central Canada	Quebec	7,237,000	7,546,000
	Ontario	11,410,000	12,160,000
Prairie Provinces	Manitoba	1,120,000	1,148,000
	Saskatchewan	979,000	968,000
	Alberta	2,975,000	3,290,000
The West Coast	British Columbia	3,908,000	4,113,000
The North	Yukon	29,000	30,000
	Northwest Territories	37,000	41,000
	Nunavut	27,000	29,000
CANADA		**30,007,000**	**31,613,000**

Source: Adapted from the Statistics Canada website, Jan. 2010, http://www12.statcan.gc.ca/census-recensement/2006/dp-pd/hlt/97-550-Index.cfm?TPL=PIC&Page=RETR&LANG=Eng&T=101.

1. Which provinces and territories increased in population from 2001 to 2006?

_____

2. Which provinces and territories decreased in population from 2001 to 2006?

_____

3. Which two provinces have the highest populations in Canada?

_____

4. Which two regions had the lowest populations in Canada in 2006?

_____

5. Which region had the highest population in Canada in 2006?

_____

Where Do Canadians Live?

Most Canadians live in the southern part of Canada, along the shaded part of the map. Most Canadians live in cities or towns.

About 30 percent of Canadians live in Canada's three largest metropolitan areas: Toronto, Montreal and Vancouver.

Canada's 10 Most Populated Metropolitan Areas*, 2006	
Toronto (ON)	5,113,149
Montreal (QC)	3,635,571
Vancouver (BC)	2,116,581
Ottawa-Gatineau (ON/QC)	1,130,761
Calgary (AB)	1,079,310
Edmonton (AB)	1,034,945
Quebec City (QC)	715,515
Winnipeg (MB)	694,668
Hamilton (ON)	692,911
London (ON)	457,720

*A Census Metropolitan Area is an area that includes a large city AND its surrounding area, which usually includes other municipalities.

Source: Adapted from the Statistics Canada website, Jan. 2010, http://www12.statcan.gc.ca/census-recensement/2006/.

Understand What You Read

(A) Map Work

On the chart, write the letter to show where each city or area is found on the map.

Most Populated Metropolitan Areas			
Toronto	*C*	Edmonton	
Montreal		Quebec City	
Vancouver		Winnipeg	
Ottawa		Hamilton	
Calgary		London	

Canadians are people from many different cultural backgrounds. Some families have lived in Canada for generations. But most Canadians have ancestors from other countries.

An **ancestor** is a relative from a long time ago, like a great-grandparent.

Aboriginal Peoples

Aboriginal peoples were the first people to live in Canada. They have lived in Canada for thousands of years. Today, about 1,200,000 Canadians are Aboriginal peoples.

People with Relatives from Other Countries

Many Canadians were born in Canada but have parents or ancestors from other countries.

The largest group of Canadians have British or French ancestors. The French and the British were the first Europeans to settle in Canada. They began to settle in Canada in the 1600s.

People from Other Countries

Many Canadians were born in other countries. They are immigrants. There are about 6 million immigrants in Canada.

Understand What You Read

(A) Discuss

1. Where were you born? _____

2. Where were your parents born? _____

3. Where were your grandparents born? _____

Interview three of your classmates. Record their answers on the chart.

Name	Where were you born?	Where were your parents born?	Where were your grandparents born?

B Match

Write the correct letter on each line to match the words with their meanings.

_____ Cultural background   a) A person who was born in one country, then moves to another country to live

_____ Ancestor   b) Your mother's or father's parent

_____ Parent   c) Time periods of about 30 years

_____ Relative   d) Your mother or your father

_____ Great-grandparent   e) The first people to live in a place

_____ Grandparent   f) A family member

_____ Aboriginals   g) Your grandparent's parent

_____ Generations   h) A relative from a long time ago

_____ Immigrant   i) Your family's or your ancestor's customs

C Answer the Questions

1. Who were the first people to live in Canada?

_____

2. Who were the first Europeans to settle in Canada?

_____

3. Who are immigrants?

_____

4. About how many immigrants are in Canada?

_____

UNIT 7
IMMIGRANTS TO CANADA

Immigration to Canada, 2008 Top 10 Source Counties	
Source Country	Number of people who became permanent residents in 2008
1. China, People's Republic of	29,300
2. India	24,500
3. Philippines	23,700
4. United States	11,200
5. United Kingdom	9,200
6. Pakistan	8,100
7. Korea, Republic of	7,200
8. France	6,400
9. Iran	6,000
10. Colombia	5,000

Source: Adapted from Facts and Figures 2008: Immigration Overview, Citizenship and Immigration Canada website, Jan. 2010, http://www.cic.gc.ca/english/resources/statistics/menu-fact.asp.

Every year about 200,000 people immigrate to Canada. An immigrant is a person who was born in one country, then moves to another country to live.

Where Do Canada's Immigrants Come From?

People immigrate to Canada from all over the world. Some immigrants have been in Canada a long time. Others immigrated to Canada recently.

Most people who immigrated to Canada before 1970 came from Europe and the United Kingdom.

Recent Immigrants

After 1970, fewer and fewer people came to Canada from Europe. More and more people immigrated from Asia and South America.

In the 1990s, many of the people who immigrated to Canada came from Asia.

Every year, thousands of people immigrate to Canada. In 2008, about 247,000 people immigrated to Canada. They came from many different countries. Over half of them came from only ten countries.

Immigrants to Canada: Top Ten Source Countries, 2008

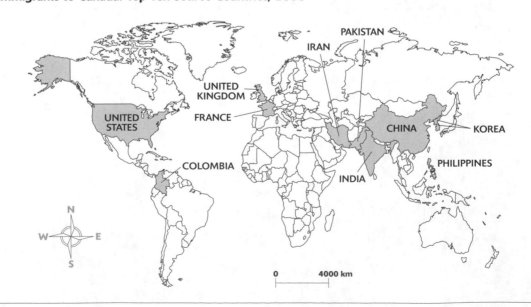

Understand What You Read

(A) Graph Work

The chart below lists the number of immigrants to Canada between 1901 and 2004.

Number of Immigrants to Canada 5-year periods, 1900 - 2004			
1900 – 1904	456,000	1955 – 1959	789,000
1905 – 1909	943,000	1960 – 1964	456,000
1910 – 1914	1,545,000	1965 – 1969	913,000
1915 – 1919	312,000	1970 – 1974	794,000
1920 – 1924	553,000	1975 – 1979	651,000
1925 – 1929	712,000	1980 – 1984	570,000
1930 – 1934	180,000	1985 – 1989	689,000
1935 – 1939	72,000	1990 – 1994	1,185,000
1940 – 1944	50,000	1995 – 1999	1,019,000
1945 – 1949	379,000	2000 – 2004	1,165,000
1950 – 1954	756,000		

Source: Adapted from Facts and Figures 2008: Immigration Overview, Citizenship and Immigration Canada. website, Jan. 2010, http://www.cic.gc.ca/english/resources/statistics/ menu-fact.asp

Shade the graph to show each five-year period. Round the number of immigrants to the nearest 100,000. The first two five-year periods are done for you.

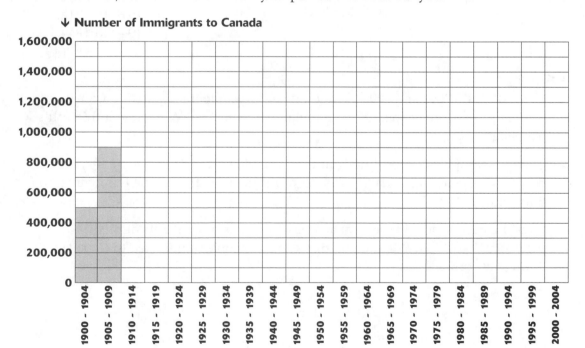

↓ **Number of Immigrants to Canada**

Discuss the graph. What does it tell you?

B Circle the Correct Answer

1. People immigrate to Canada from
   a) all over the world.
   b) only ten countries.
   c) Canada.

2. Most people who immigrated to Canada before 1970 were
   a) from Asia.
   b) from Africa.
   c) from Europe.

3. Most people who immigrated to Canada in the 1990s were
   a) from Asia.
   b) from Africa.
   c) from Europe.

4. In 2008, the largest group of immigrants came from
   a) the United States.
   b) India.
   c) China.

Look at the graph you drew on the previous page. Since 1900,

5. Canada accepted the most immigrants during the years
   a) 1995 to 1999.
   b) 1910 to 1914.
   c) 1940 to 1944.

6. Canada accepted the fewest immigrants during the years
   a) 1995 to 1999.
   b) 1910 to 1914.
   c) 1940 to 1944.

C Discuss

1. In the 1970s, 1980s and 1990s, fewer and fewer people immigrated to Canada from Europe. More people started immigrating from Asia. Why do you think this happened?

2. Canada accepted the most immigrants in a single year in 1913, when 400,870 people immigrated to Canada. Why do you think so many people immigrated to Canada in 1913?

3. Over the past hundred years, Canada had the fewest immigrants during the period 1940 to 1944. Why do you think so few people immigrated to Canada during this time?

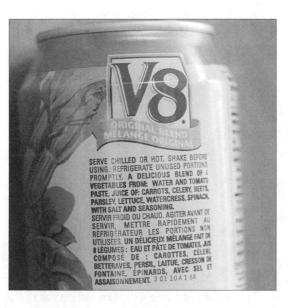

Canada's Official Languages

An **official language** is the language the government uses. Canada has two official languages, English and French.

A Bilingual Canada

Canada is bilingual. Bilingual means **speaking two languages**. Canadians can get information and services from the government of Canada in English or French.

All products sold in Canada must have information in French and English on the package.

Canada's Other Languages

The first language a person learns and still understands is called his or her **mother tongue**. The mother tongue of most Canadians is English or French. But many Canadians first learned other languages. Here are the top ten mother-tongue languages of Canadians.

Most Common Mother-Tongue Languages (Canada, 2006) 2006 population: about 31,000,000	
Language	**Number of people**
English	17,883,000
French	6,818,000
Chinese languages	1,012,000
Italian	455,000
German	451,000
Punjabi	368,000
Spanish	345,000
Arabic	262,000
Tagalog	236,000
Portuguese	219,000

Source: Adapted from the Statistics Canada website, Jan 2010, http://www40.statcan.ca/l01/cst01/demo11a-eng.htm.

In the 2006 census, about 58 percent of Canadians reported English as their mother tongue.

About 22 percent reported French as their mother tongue.

Understand What You Read

(A) Answer the Questions

1. What are Canada's two official languages?

_____

2. What is an official language?

_____

3. What is a mother tongue?

_____

4. What does **bilingual** mean?

_____

5. Match the boxes to make a sentence.

About 58 percent of Canadians'	**in Canada are Chinese languages.**
About 22 percent of Canadians'	**mother tongue is English.**
About 20 percent of Canadians'	**mother tongue is a non-official language.**
The most common non-official language(s)	**mother tongue is French.**

(B) Discuss

1. How many languages can you speak?

2. What is your mother tongue?

3. Interview three classmates. Record their answers on the chart below.

Names	What languages can you speak?	What is your mother tongue?

Canadians and Work

In Units nine to thirteen, you will learn about Canadians and their work.

Before you work on the units, try to answer the following questions.

1. What kinds of jobs do you think most Canadians have?

2. What is the minimum wage in your province? In Canada, do you think most workers make more than the minimum wage?

3. What do you think is the average hourly wage in Canada?

4. What hourly wage do you think is necessary for a person to live comfortably in Canada?

5. Do you think many Canadians are unemployed?

6. Which areas of Canada do you think have high unemployment rates?

UNIT 9
CANADA'S CURRENCY

Canada's currency includes six coins and five bills. The Royal Canadian Mint makes Canada's coins. The Bank of Canada makes our bills. The Royal Canadian Mint and the Bank of Canada are government corporations.

Canada's Coins

All of Canada's coins have a portrait of Queen Elizabeth II on one side. The other side of each coin has a picture that symbolizes Canada. The $1 and $2 coins, the 25-cent coin and the 5-cent coin have pictures of animals that are common in Canada. They symbolize our wildlife.

Canada's Bills

Canada has five bills. The $5, $10, $50 and $100 bills have a portrait of a former prime minister on them. Canada's first prime minister is pictured on the $10 bill. The $20 bill has a portrait of Queen Elizabeth II on it.

Understand What You Read

(A) Fill in the Blanks

Look at Canada's bills. Describe the pictures on the back of each bill. You can find pictures of the bills on the Bank of Canada website (www.bankofcanada.ca), under *bank notes*.

	On the Front	On the Back
$5 bill	Sir Wilfrid Laurier	
$10 bill	Sir John A. Macdonald	
$20 bill	Queen Elizabeth II	
$50 bill	William Lyon Mackenzie King	
$100 bill	Sir Robert Borden	

B Crossword

Try to complete the crossword without using the word list. If it is difficult, use the word list.

DOWN ↓
1. The colour of our $20 bill
2. Pictured on our 10-cent coin
3. Pictured on our $2 coin
4. Pictured on our 1-cent coin
5. The colour of our $5 bill
6. Makes Canada's bills
7. Common name for our 25-cent coin
8. Common name for our $1 coin
9. Common name for our 10-cent coin
10. Pictured on our 25-cent coin
11. Makes Canada's coins

ACROSS →
12. Pictured on our 5-cent coin
13. The first name of the Queen
14. Pictured on Canada's $5 bill
15. Common name for our $2 coin
16. Common name for our 5-cent coin
17. Pictured on our $10 bill
18. The colour of our $100 bill
19. Common name for our 1-cent coin
20. The colour of Canada's $50 bill
21. The colour of our $10 bill
22. Pictured on our $1 coin

Word List

Royal Canadian Mint • penny • caribou • dime • loon
nickel • green • red • loonie • brown • beaver • Elizabeth
schooner • Bank of Canada • purple • polar bear • Macdonald
toonie • quarter • maple leaf • Laurier • blue

C Word Match

Draw a line to match each word with its meaning.

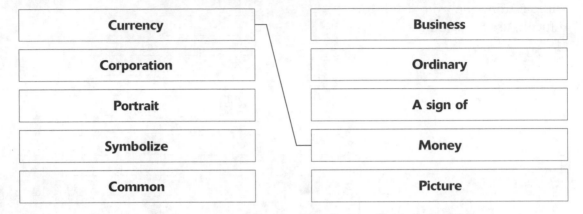

Currency	Business
Corporation	Ordinary
Portrait	A sign of
Symbolize	Money
Common	Picture

D Answer the Questions

1. What organization makes Canada's coins?

_____

2. Who is pictured on all of Canada's coins?

_____

3. Who is pictured on Canada's $20 bill?

_____

4. Which bill has a picture of Canada's first prime minister on it?

_____

5. Who was Canada's first prime minister?

_____

6. How many types of coins do we use in Canada?

_____

7. How many types of bills do we use in Canada?

_____

E Discuss

1. How are Canada's bills different from the bills in your country of origin?

2. How are Canada's coins different from the coins in your country of origin?

3. What do you like (or dislike) about Canada's currency?

CANADIANS AND JOB INDUSTRIES

What Is an Industry?

Canadians work at many different kinds of jobs. An industry is a type of business. Three important industries in Canada are the natural resource industry, the manufacturing industry and the service industry.

Natural resource industry jobs take objects from nature that we can use. Manufacturing industry jobs make these things into products we can buy and use. Service industry jobs sell these products and services to people.

The Natural Resource Industry

Natural resources are things like forests, oceans and lakes, rock and soil. They are things in nature that we can use. People who work in the natural resource industry catch fish, cut down trees, work in mines and farm the land.

The Manufacturing Industry

The manufacturing industry uses things from the natural resource industry to make the products we buy and use every day. Some of these products are paper, food, cars, furniture and tools. Many people who work in the manufacturing industry have jobs in factories.

The Service Industry

The service industry serves people what they want or need. The service industry includes jobs in stores, restaurants, hotels, schools, hospitals, construction companies, government agencies and banks. Most workers in Canada work in the service industry.

There are about 17 million workers in Canada. Most of them work in the service industry.

Understand What You Read

A) Sort

Write each word under its correct heading.

> waiter • fisher • factory worker • miner • water
> bank teller • forest • hair stylist • rock • furniture maker
> logger • plant manager

Natural Resources

_____

_____

_____

Natural Resource Industry Jobs

_____

_____

_____

Manufacturing Industry Jobs

_____

_____

_____

Service Industry Jobs

_____

_____

_____

B) Match

Draw a line to match each item with its description.

Primary industry jobs	things in nature we can use.
Manufacturing industry jobs	provide people with things they want.
Service industry jobs	make things we buy and use every day.
Natural resources are	mountains, oceans, rock and forest.
Some natural resources are	take things from nature.

C) Discuss

1. What industry do you work in?

2. What industry would you like to work in? Why?

UNIT 11
THE MINIMUM WAGE

What Is the Minimum Wage?

The minimum wage is the lowest hourly wage an employer can pay you. An employer can pay you more, but cannot pay you less than the minimum wage.

The government of each province and territory decides on its own minimum wage.

In some provinces, there is a separate minimum wage for students and liquor servers. For example, Ontario's minimum wage is $9.50 (as of Jan. 2010). For Ontario students under 18 years of age, the minimum wage is $8.90. For Ontario liquor servers, the minimum wage is $8.25.

Do Many People Make the Minimum Wage?

Most workers make more than the minimum wage. The average wage in Canada is about $22 an hour.

Minimum Wages in Canada (as of Jan. 2010)	
Province	**Per Hour**
British Columbia	$8.00
Alberta	$8.80
Saskatchewan	$9.25
Manitoba	$9.00
Ontario	$9.50
Quebec	$9.00
Nova Scotia	$8.60
New Brunswick	$8.25
Prince Edward Island	$8.40
Newfoundland and Labrador	$9.50
Nunavut	$10.00
Northwest Territories	$8.25
Yukon	$8.89

Source: Current and Forthcoming Minimum Hourly Wage Rates, for Experienced Adult Workers in Canada, Jan. 2010, http://srv116.services.gc.ca/ dimt-wid/sm-mw/rpt1.aspx?lang=eng.

Understand What You Read

A Discuss

1. Why do you think some provinces have higher minimum wages than other provinces?

2. Do you think Canada's minimum wages are enough to live on?

3. Why do you think the student minimum wage in Ontario is less than the adult minimum wage?

4. In Ontario, why do you think the minimum wage for liquor servers is lower than the regular minimum wage?

B) Correct the Sentence

Each sentence below is false. Change the underlined word to write a correct sentence on each line.

1. The minimum wage is the <u>highest</u> wage an employer can pay you.

The minimum wage is the lowest wage an employer can pay you.

2. Ontario's student minimum wage is <u>higher</u> than the adult minimum wage.

_____

3. <u>All</u> workers make more than the minimum wage.

_____

4. The average wage in Canada is about <u>$12</u> an hour.

_____

5. <u>Alberta</u> has the highest minimum wage in Canada.

_____

6. <u>Quebec</u> has the lowest minimum wage in Canada.

_____

C) Vocabulary Match

Write the correct words beside their meanings.

alcohol • normal • boss • pay • lowest • different • per hour

minimum   _____   separate   _____

hourly   _____   liquor   _____

wage   _____   average   _____

employer   _____

D Answer the Questions

1. Which two Canadian provinces have the highest minimum wages?

_____

2. Which province has the lowest minimum wage?

_____

3. Which two provinces have the same minimum wage?

_____

4. Which territory has the highest territorial minimum wage?

_____

5. Who decides what the minimum wage will be?

_____

E Discuss

1. Which kinds of jobs do you think pay the minimum wage?

2. What is the minimum wage in the province you live in?

3. Do you think the minimum wage should be higher? Why?

4. Is there a minimum wage law in your country of origin?

EARNINGS AND DEDUCTIONS

Employees usually get paid every two weeks. Most employees receive a pay stub with their pay. A pay stub tells you how much you earned and how much money was deducted from your pay. Deductions are amounts of money subtracted from our earnings. Usually, the biggest deduction is for income tax. CPP and EI payments are also deducted from our pay.

Tax

A tax is an amount of money that goes to the government. People who own property in Canada pay tax every year. This tax is called property tax. We pay tax on the goods and services we buy every day. This tax is called sales tax. Workers pay tax on the money they earn. This tax is called income tax.

The government gets most of its money from taxes. The government uses tax money to pay for services Canadians need, such as health care, welfare, government pensions and schools.

Canadian workers also pay some of their income to the government's Canada Pension Plan and Employment Insurance program.

CPP

CPP stands for **Canadian Pension Plan**. CPP payments from workers help the government pay our CPP pension when we reach the age of 65.

EI

EI stands for **Employment Insurance**. EI is a government program that helps people who lose their jobs, have to stop working to have a baby or have to stop working because they get injured. EI payments from workers help to pay for the EI program.

Usually, income tax, CPP and EI payments are deducted from our pay cheques.

A pay stub looks something like this:

PAY STUB			
Employee Name: John Simon		**Deductions**	
Hourly Rate:	$13.00	**Total Income Tax:**	$150.00
Hours Worked:	80 hours	**Canada Pension Plan:**	$42.50
		Employment Insurance:	$22.90
Gross Pay:	$1,040.00	**Total Deductions:**	$215.40
		Net Pay:	$824.60

Understand What You Read

(A) Match

Write the correct letter on the lines to match the words with their meanings.

_____ Employment Insurance   a) Pay before deductions

_____ Canada Pension Plan   b) Pay after deductions

_____ Gross pay   c) A weekly payment for people who have lost their jobs

_____ Net pay   d) A monthly payment for Canadians aged 65 and older who have worked in Canada

_____ Pay stub   e) An amount of money subtracted from a pay cheque

_____ Deduction   f) Lists your earnings and deductions

(B) Answer the Questions

1. Look at the pay stub on the previous page. Fill in the blanks below with the information on the pay stub.

   Pay per hour: _____

   Hours worked: _____

   Gross pay: _____

   Income tax: _____

   CPP: _____

   EI: _____

   Net pay: _____

2. List three different kinds of taxes we pay in Canada.

   _____

3. List three things the government spends tax money on.

   _____

UNIT 13
UNEMPLOYMENT

Unemployment Rates in Canada (for November 2009)	
British Columbia	8.3%
Alberta	7.5%
Saskatchewan	5.2%
Manitoba	5.8%
Ontario	9.3%
Quebec	8.1%
New Brunswick	8.8%
Nova Scotia	9.5%
Prince Edward Island	11.7%
Newfoundland and Labrador	15.9%

Source: Adapted from the Statistics Canada website, Jan. 2010, http://www40.statcan.gc.ca/101/cst01/lfss01a-eng.htm.

People are employed if they have a job. If they do not have a job, they are unemployed.

In Canada, about 17 million people 15 years of age and older are employed. Many others want to work but cannot find a job.

The Unemployment Rate

The unemployment rate tells us how many people are looking for a job but cannot find one.

If the unemployment rate is 10 percent, it means that 10 out of 100 people cannot find a job. The unemployment rate is different for each province.

Understand What You Read

(A) Answer the Questions

1. In November 2009, which three provinces had the lowest unemployment rates?

   _____

2. In which region are these provinces (the North, the West Coast, the Prairie provinces or the Atlantic region)?

   _____

3. In November 2009, which four provinces had the highest unemployment rates?

   _____

4. In which regions are these provinces?

   _____

5. Which is better: a high unemployment rate or a low unemployment rate?

   _____

PART **TWO - THE PEOPLE**

B Map Work

Write the correct unemployment rate (for November 2009) in each box.

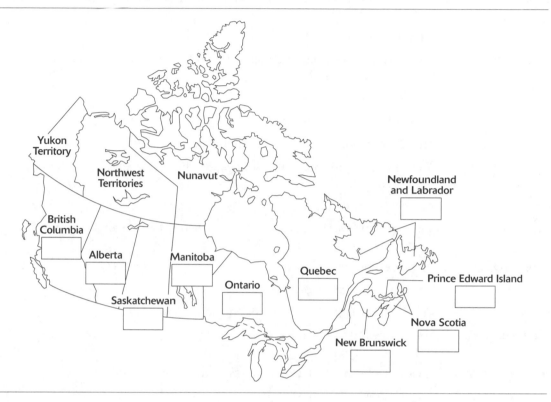

C Partner Activity

1. One student works with Chart A; the other with Chart B. Students question each other to fill in the missing information.

Chart A Canada's Unemployment Rate	
1992	
1996	9.6%
2000	
2004	7.2%
2006	

Chart B Canada's Unemployment Rate	
1992	11.2%
1996	
2000	6.8%
2004	
2006	6.1%

Source: Adapted from the Statistics Canada website, Jan. 2010, http://www4.hrsdc.gc.ca/.3ndic.1t.4r@-eng.jsp?iid=16#M_1.

2. Students describe how the unemployment rate has changed in Canada since 1992.

THE PEOPLE

Ancestor:	A relative from a long time ago, like a great-grandparent
Bank of Canada:	A government bank that helps to keep Canada's economy healthy and also makes Canada's bills
Bilingual:	Having two languages
Canada Pension Plan:	A government pension for Canadians who have worked in Canada and have reached the age of 65
Census:	An official count of the population
Currency:	Types of bills and coins that make up a money system
Deductions:	Amounts of money subtracted from income
Employment Insurance:	A government program that helps people who lose their job (when it is not their fault)
Gross pay:	Income before deductions
Immigrant:	Someone who was born in one country, then moved to another country to live
Manufacturing industry:	Includes jobs that produce the things we buy and use every day
Minimum wage:	The lowest hourly wage an employer can pay you
Mother tongue:	The first language a person learns and still understands
Natural resource:	Something found in nature that can be used, like water, forests, minerals or fish
Natural resource industry:	Includes jobs that extract natural resources from the land
Net pay:	Income after deductions
Official language:	The language the government uses
Pension:	Money paid regularly to a person, usually after he or she turns 65
Population:	The number of people living in a country or area
Property tax:	A yearly tax we pay for living on property
Royal Canadian Mint:	Makes Canada's coins
Sales tax:	A tax on products and services we buy
Service industry:	Includes jobs that serve people with the things they want
Statistics Canada:	Offers information about the results of the census
Taxes:	Amounts of money (on income, property and products) that go to the government
Unemployment rate:	The number of unemployed people for every 100 adults who are looking for work

PART 3
THE HISTORY

Canada's History

Get Ready to Learn		**78**
Unit 1	Aboriginal Peoples	**79**
Unit 2	New France	**82**
Unit 3	British Rule	**84**
Unit 4	Confederation	**87**
Unit 5	Aboriginal Peoples and European Settlement	**90**
Unit 6	Settling the West	**92**
Unit 7	Canada and the World Wars	**94**
Unit 8	The Constitution Act	**96**
Unit 9	The Canadian Charter of Rights and Freedoms	**98**
Unit 10	Celebrating Our History: Victoria Day	**100**
Unit 11	Celebrating Our History: Canada Day	**102**
Unit 12	Celebrating Our History: Aboriginal Peoples	**104**
Glossary		**105**

In Units one to twelve, you will learn a little about Canada's history.

Before you work on the units, try to answer these questions.

1. When do you think Canada became an independent country?

2. A thousand years ago, who do you think lived in Canada?

3. How do you think these people lived?

4. When do you think Europeans first visited Canada?

5. When Europeans started to settle in Canada, how do you think they got along with the people who were already living there?

6. How do you think they helped each other?

7. How do you think they hurt each other?

8. How do you think the early settlers survived in Canada?

9. Which country do you think first claimed Canada as its colony?

10. Two countries went to war over parts of Canada's land. Which two countries were they?

ABORIGINAL PEOPLES

Aboriginal peoples were the first people to live in Canada. They are also called Native peoples. They lived in Canada for thousands of years before Europeans arrived.

There are three groups of Aboriginal peoples: the North American Indians, the Inuit and the Métis.

The North American Indians

North American Indians are sometimes called the First Nations, Native peoples or Indians. North American Indians lived all over Canada.

There are many different groups of North American Indians. These groups are called **bands**. Different bands speak different languages.

About 700,000 North American Indians live in Canada today.

The Inuit

The Inuit are Aboriginal people who mostly live in northern areas of Canada. They are also called **Eskimos** or **Native peoples**.

About 50,000 Inuit people live in Canada today. Most Inuit speak the language called Inuktitut. **Inuit** means **the people** in Inuktitut. Many Inuit people live in Nunavut. **Nunavut** means **our land** in Inuktitut.

The Métis

Métis means **mixed**. Thousands of years after the Inuit and the North American Indians had been in Canada, Europeans arrived. Some Europeans had children with the North American Indians. These children and their families are called the Métis people.

About 390,000 Métis live in Canada today.

Understand What You Read

Aboriginal Population in Canada, 2006				
Region		North American Indian	Métis	Inuit
Atlantic Region	Newfoundland and Labrador	7,765	6,470	4,715
	Prince Edward Island	1,225	385	30
	Nova Scotia	15,240	7,680	325
	New Brunswick	12,385	4,270	185
Central Canada	Quebec	65,085	27,980	10,950
	Ontario	158,395	73,605	2,035
Prairie Provinces	Manitoba	100,640	71,805	565
	Saskatchewan	91,400	48,120	215
	Alberta	97,275	85,495	1,610
The West Coast	British Columbia	129,580	59,445	795
The North	Yukon	6,280	800	255
	Northwest Territories	12,640	5,580	4,160
	Nunavut	100	130	24,635
TOTAL IN CANADA		**698,025**	**389,780**	**50,480**

Source: Adapted from the Statistics Canada website, Jan. 2010, http://www12.statcan.ca/censusrecensement/2006/.

(A) Answer the Questions

1. In which region do most Inuit people live?

_____

2. In which region do most Métis people live?

_____

3. In which two regions do most North American Indians live?

_____

4. Many Inuit live in the northern area of two provinces. Name the provinces.

_____

5. About how many Aboriginal peoples (in total) live in Canada?

_____

6. How many North American Indians live in Canada?

_____

7. How many Inuit live in Canada?

_____

8. How many Métis live in Canada?

_____

B Match

Write the correct letter on the lines to match the words with their meanings.

_____ Nunavut   a) A group of North American Indian people

_____ Aboriginal people   b) An Aboriginal people living mostly in
                                               northern Canada

_____ Inuit   c) The language of the Inuit

_____ Band   d) Another name for North American Indians

_____ Inuktitut   e) Means the first people to live in a place

_____ Métis   f) Means **our land** in Inuktitut

_____ Eskimo   g) Another word for the Inuit

_____ First Nations   h) People who have a mix of Aboriginal and
                                               European ancestors.

C Correct the Sentences

These sentences are false. Change the underlined word to correct the sentences.

1. The Inuit are sometimes called <u>Métis</u>.

_____

2. North American Indians are also called <u>Eskimos</u>.

_____

3. <u>Europeans</u> were the first people to live in Canada.

_____

4. <u>North American Indians</u> live mostly in northern Canada.

_____

D Discuss

Is there an Aboriginal population in your country of origin? What do you know
about them?

UNIT 2
NEW FRANCE

Thousands of years after Aboriginal people lived in Canada, European explorers arrived in Canada. They sailed to eastern Canada from Norway, Sweden, Denmark, Spain, England and France.

One famous French explorer was Jacques Cartier. He sailed to eastern Canada in 1534. He learned that the Aboriginal word for village was **Kanata.** Many people think this is why our country is called Canada.

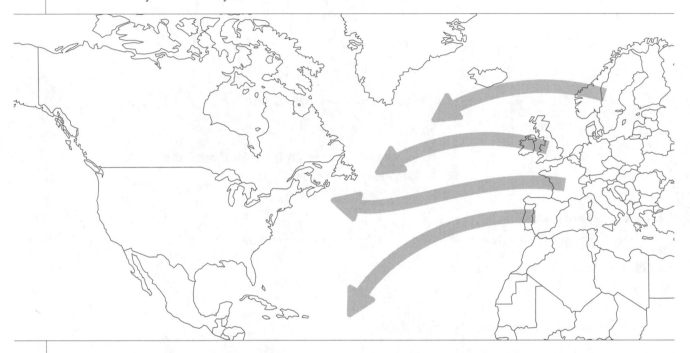

French Settlement in the 1500s, 1600s and 1700s

The French government wanted eastern Canada to be its colony. France sent people to live in Canada. French people settled in parts of the Atlantic Region and Quebec. The French government called the settlements **New France**.

What Did the Settlers Do?

Some settlers farmed the land. Others traded with Aboriginal peoples. The most important trade was in beaver furs. Europeans wanted beaver furs to make hats. Aboriginal people wanted tools, weapons and cloth.

Some French fur traders had children with Aboriginal people. Their children and descendants are called the Métis people.

By the 1700s, thousands of French settlers lived in New France. Most of them lived in southern Quebec.

Understand What You Read

(A) Match

Write the correct letter on the lines to match the words with their meanings.

_____ New France   a) A famous French explorer

_____ Colony   b) French colonies in Canada

_____ Beaver furs   c) People who move to a new undeveloped land to live

_____ Settlers   d) Land a country owns that is far away

_____ Jacques Cartier   e) Used to make hats in Europe

(B) Answer the Questions

1. Where were the early European explorers from?

_____

2. When did Jacques Cartier sail to Canada?

_____

3. Where did the word **Canada** come from?

_____

4. Why did the French government want people to settle in Canada?

_____

5. What did France call its colonies in Canada?

_____

6. Where did the French people settle in Canada?

_____

7. What did the French people do in Canada?

_____

(C) Discuss

1. Why do you think countries want colonies? Was your country of origin a colony?

2. How do you think Aboriginal people felt when Europeans came to Canada?

BRITISH RULE

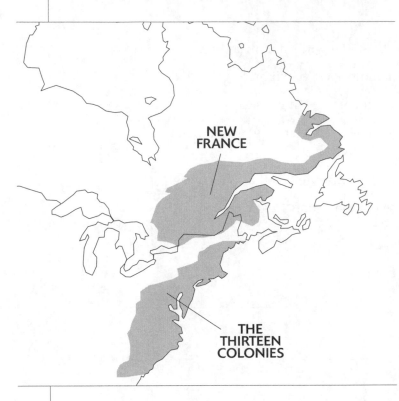

NEW FRANCE

THE THIRTEEN COLONIES

French and British Settlement

When French people were settling in Canada, British people were settling in parts of the United States. At that time, thirteen parts of the eastern United States were colonies of Britain. They were loosely called the **thirteen** colonies.

In the 1700s, Britain wanted to own the colonies in Canada, too. At that time, the colonies in parts of Canada were owned by France. They were called New France.

France and England at War

France and England both wanted to own parts of Canada. They went to war. In 1763, England won the war. The French colonies in Canada became British colonies. Britain called the colonies British North America.

The French people wanted to keep their language and customs. The British government agreed. A law called the **Quebec Act** described how the French people's way of life would be protected.

More British People Came to Canada

Later, more and more British people came to Canada. They came from England, Ireland, Scotland and Wales. Other British people came from what is now the United States.

Why Did People Move to Canada from the United States?

Most of the people in the thirteen colonies wanted to be independent from Britain. In 1776, they became independent. The colonies became the United States of America, or the U.S.A. But some British people there didn't want independence. They wanted to stay loyal to England. They were called **Loyalists**. Many Loyalists came to Canada because Canada was still a British colony. Most of them moved to Ontario and the Atlantic provinces.

The French and the British in Canada

There were many conflicts between the French and the British in Canada. They spoke two different languages. They had different customs and different religions.

Today, there are still conflicts between French-speaking and English-speaking Canada.

Understand What You Read

© PEARSON LONGMAN • REPRODUCTION PROHIBITED

(A) Circle the Correct Answer

1. Before 1763, French settlements in Canada were called
   a) the thirteen colonies.
   b) Canada.
   c) New France.

2. British settlements in the United States were called
   a) the thirteen colonies.
   b) Canada.
   c) New France.

3. New France became a British colony in
   a) 1776.
   b) 1763.
   c) 1534.

4. The thirteen colonies became independent from Britain in
   a) 1776.
   b) 1763.
   c) 1534.

5. The Loyalists came to Canada because they wanted
   a) independence.
   b) to live in the United States.
   c) to remain British.

(B) Fill in the Blanks

| colony • New France • United States • thirteen |
| independent • French • language • British |

1. Before 1763, parts of Canada were _____ colonies.

2. The French colonies in Canada were called _____.

3. Parts of the United States were _____ colonies.

4. There were _____ British colonies in the United States.

5. In 1763, New France became a British _____.

6. When New France became British, French people were afraid of losing their

   _____.

7. In 1776, the thirteen colonies became _____ from Britain.

8. After 1776, the thirteen colonies became the _____.

C Answer the Questions

1. Why did France and England go to war in Canada?

_____

2. Who won the war?

_____

3. When did the French colonies become British colonies?

_____

4. What did Britain call its new colony in what is now Canada?

_____

5. What law made sure French people in Canada could keep their language and customs?

_____

6. When did the thirteen colonies become independent from Britain?

_____

7. Why did the Loyalists come to Canada?

_____

8. Where did the Loyalists come to Canada from?

_____

9. Where in British North America did the Loyalists settle?

_____

10. After Canada became a British colony, more English-speaking people came to Canada. Where did they come from?

_____

D Discuss

Today, Canada is officially bilingual. Canada's languages are English and French. Do you think it is important for all Canadians to learn to speak French and English? Why?

Canada Wants Independence

In the 1800s, more and more people settled in different parts of Canada. Canada was owned by Britain and was called British North America.

Canadian leaders talked about bringing the areas of British North America together. They talked about becoming independent from Britain. They talked about having their own government.

The leaders wanted one government for all of Canada. But each area in Canada had different concerns. Because of this, they decided that each area would also have a smaller government of its own. The government of Canada would be the **federal** government. The smaller governments in each area would be **provincial** governments. The ideas about governing Canada were written down. Canadian leaders hoped the ideas would become law.

The British Government Agrees

The British government listened to Canadian leaders. In 1867, the British government made the ideas into law for Canada. The law was called the **British North America Act**, or the BNA Act.

The First Provinces of Canada

On July 1, 1867, Ontario, Quebec, Nova Scotia and New Brunswick became the first provinces of Canada. We call this historic event **Confederation**. Confederation happens when different areas come together, or unite.

Canada Governs Itself

In 1867, Sir John A. Macdonald became Canada's first prime minister. The prime minister is the person who leads the federal government. Macdonald's picture is on our $10 bill.

Other Provinces and Territories Join Confederation

Later, other provinces and the territories joined Canada. Manitoba and the Northwest Territories joined three years after Confederation in 1870. British Columbia joined in 1871. Prince Edward Island joined in 1873. Yukon Territory joined in 1898. Saskatchewan and Alberta joined in 1905. Newfoundland and Labrador joined in 1949. Nunavut joined in 1999. (Prior to 1999, Nunavut was part of the Northwest Territories.)

Understand What You Read

A Answer the Questions

1. When did Canada become independent?

_____

2. List the first provinces that were part of Canada.

_____

3. Who was Canada's first prime minister?

_____

4. Which country owned Canada before Confederation?

_____

5. What does the word **confederation** mean?

_____

6. What was the BNA Act?

_____

7. Which province was the last to join Confederation?

_____

B Fill in the Blanks

Write the year each province joined Confederation. Shade the first four provinces of Canada on the map.

Ontario _____

Quebec _____

Nova Scotia _____

New Brunswick _____

Manitoba _____

Northwest Territories _____

British Columbia _____

Prince Edward Island _____

Yukon Territory _____

Saskatchewan _____

Alberta _____

Newfoundland
and Labrador _____

Nunavut _____

C Crossword

Complete the crossword.

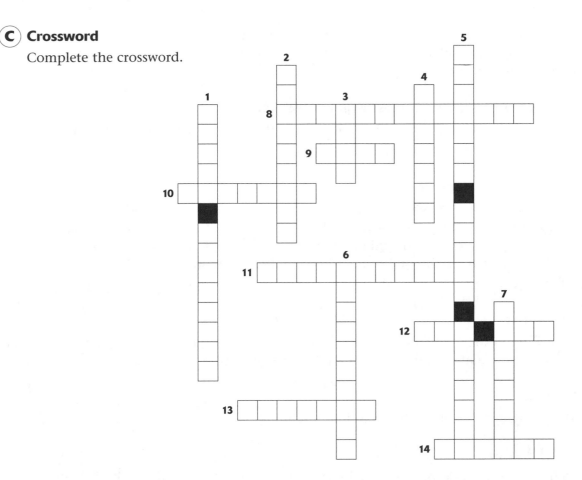

DOWN ↓

1. The leader of Canada's federal government
2. The last name of Canada's first prime minister
3. In 1867, ____ provinces joined Canada.
4. Before 1867, ____ owned Canada.
5. The name of British-owned areas of Canada
6. The ____ government governs a province.
7. ____ joined Canada in 1870.

ACROSS →

8. ____ means to unite.
9. Canada became independent in the month of ____.
10. The ____ government governs all of Canada.
11. A self-governing country
12. The law that listed the first rules of Canada's government
13. One of the first provinces of Canada
14. The name of British North America after it became independent

Word List

four • Canada • Confederation • July • prime minister
Macdonald • Ontario • BNA Act • independent • Manitoba
Britain • federal • British North America • provincial

ABORIGINAL PEOPLES AND
EUROPEAN SETTLEMENT

Aboriginal peoples lived in Canada long before the first Europeans arrived. There were many groups of Aboriginal peoples. They lived all over Canada. They survived by hunting, fishing and growing crops.

Contact with Europeans Brings Problems

Europeans and Aboriginal people learned many things from each other. But they also had many problems.

Fighting between Bands

Europeans traded with Aboriginal people. Europeans wanted beaver and buffalo furs. In Europe, the beaver furs were used to make hats. In return, Europeans gave Aboriginal people weapons, tools, cloth and other items. This exchange was called the **fur trade**. The fur trade grew. There were fights between different groups of Aboriginal groups. They fought over hunting land.

Disease

When Europeans came to Canada, some of them had contagious diseases. The diseases spread to Aboriginal people. Many Aboriginal people died from the diseases.

Land Loss

Many Aboriginal people lost the land they had lived on.

Assimilation

Many Europeans thought Aboriginal people should be more like them. They tried to teach Aboriginal people European ways of thinking. They tried to convert them to Christianity. Because of this, many Aboriginal people lost their way of life, their language and their culture.

Aboriginal Peoples Are Still Struggling

Later, Canada started respecting the rights of Aboriginal people.

Even today, Aboriginal people are fighting to get back to and to keep their land, their culture and their power.

Understand What You Read

A **Answer the Questions**

1. How did Aboriginal people survive in Canada?

   _____

2. Europeans caused some problems for Aboriginal people. List four problems.

   _____

3. What was the fur trade?

   _____

4. The fur trade was important to Canada's economy in the 1700s. What Canadian coin reminds us of the fur trade?

   _____

5. What did the European traders give to Aboriginal people in return for beaver furs?

   _____

6. What did Europeans do with the beaver furs?

   _____

7. How did the fur trade hurt Aboriginal people?

   _____

8. How do you think the fur trade helped Aboriginal people?

   _____

B **Discuss**

European settlement in Canada caused many problems for Aboriginal people. Do you think these problems could have been avoided? How?

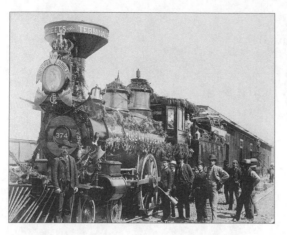

Canada Builds a Railway

In 1867, Canada became a country with four provinces: Ontario, Quebec, Nova Scotia and New Brunswick. Manitoba joined three years later in 1870.

The Canadian government wanted Canada to reach from the Atlantic Ocean to the Pacific Ocean. Canada asked British Columbia to join Confederation. British Columbia said it would join, but only if Canada built a railway.

Why Did British Columbia Want a Railway?

British Columbia was very far from the other provinces. The people who lived there felt isolated. A railway would bring them the things they needed for their daily lives.

Canada agreed to build the railway. It was finished in 1885.

Canada Wants More People

In 1885, Canada had a lot of land and a railway but the country needed more people. Canada promised people free land in western Canada. Many people moved to western Canada and took the land. Between 1901 and 1911, Canada grew by almost two million people! Because of this, the government created two new western provinces, Alberta and Saskatchewan.

Aboriginal Peoples

North American Indians and Métis already lived in the West. They were angry because Canada was giving away land they lived on. The government set up areas of land, called reserves, for Aboriginal people to live on. Aboriginal people didn't like this. They wanted their way of life to stay the same.

Understand What You Read

(A) Fill in the Blanks

| people • reserves • free • grew • railway |
| completed • reserve • land • upset |

1. A _____ is land saved for aboriginal people.

2. British Columbia agreed to join Confederation if Canada built a _____.

3. The railway was _____ in 1885.

4. Canada had a lot of land, but it wanted more _____.

5. Canada promised people _____ land if they settled in western Canada.

6. Between 1901 and 1911, Canada _____ by almost two million people.

7. Aboriginal people in western Canada were _____.

8. Canada was giving away the _____ the Aboriginal people lived on.

9. Canada set up _____ for some Aboriginal groups.

(B) Discuss

1. How do you think a railway helps a country grow?

2. Would you move to a new country if the government gave you free land?
   Discuss the advantages and disadvantages of becoming a settler in a new country.

3. Why do you think Aboriginal people did not like the reserves?

CANADA AND THE WORLD WARS

World War I Memorial

World War I

In 1914, Britain declared war on Germany. This was the beginning of the First World War. World War I ended on November 11, 1918.

Canada supported Britain in the war. Thousands of Canadians went to Europe to fight. More than 60,000 Canadians died in World War I.

The Peace Tower was built to honour the Canadians killed in World War I. The tower stands in front of the Parliament Buildings in Ottawa.

November 11 is Remembrance Day. On Remembrance Day, we remember Canadians who died fighting in wars.

World War II

In 1939, Britain and France declared war on Germany. This was the beginning of World War II. The war ended in 1945.

Canada supported Britain and declared war on Germany, too. More than one million Canadians fought in the war. About 42,000 Canadians died in World War II.

After the Wars

After the world wars, Canada's population grew. Many Europeans immigrated to Canada. Canadian women started having more babies. We call the years that followed the Second World War the **baby boom**.

During and after the wars, the Canadian government started some important programs we still have today: employment insurance, old age pensions, family allowance payments and universal health care.

Understand What You Read

(A) **Discuss**

1. Do you think it is a good idea to have an official day to remember wars and the people who died in them? Why?

2. What do you think of Canada's social programs?

B Match

Write the correct letter on each line to match the words to their meanings.

_____ Declared   a) Moved to a different country

_____ Supported   b) The years during which many women
                                            had babies

_____ Immigrated   c) Monthly payments to seniors

_____ Baby boom   d) Helped

_____ Employment Insurance   e) For everyone

_____ Old age pension   f) Honours the Canadians killed in the
                                            First World War

_____ Universal   g) Payments to people who lose their jobs

_____ The Peace Tower   h) Officially said

C Answer the Questions

1. When did the First World War end?

_____

2. When is Remembrance Day?

_____

3. Why was the Peace Tower built?

_____

4. Where is the Peace Tower?

_____

5. About how many Canadians died during the First and Second World Wars?

_____

6. List three programs the Canadian government started after the wars.

_____

Before 1867, Canada was a British colony called British North America.

In 1867, the British government let Canada govern itself. But the British government still had some power in Canada. Canada could not change the BNA Act without permission from the British government. The BNA Act listed Canada's most important laws.

As time passed, Canadians wanted to be even more independent from Britain. In 1982, Canada became more self-governing. Canada could change its laws without asking Britain first.

How Did It Happen?

In 1982, Canadian leaders made some changes to the BNA Act. Here are three important changes:

1. They changed the name of the BNA Act to the Constitution Act.

2. Canadian leaders thought all Canadians should be free and that the law should treat everyone equally. They wrote a list of the most important rights everyone should have. The list was called the **Charter of Rights and Freedoms**. They added the Charter of Rights and Freedoms to the Constitution Act so the rights would be law.

3. Canadians thought that Canada should be free to make and change its laws about government without asking Britain.

The British government agreed with the changes. Canada's prime minister and the Queen of England signed their names. This made the changes legal. Pierre Elliott Trudeau was Canada's prime minister.

Understand What You Read

© PEARSON LONGMAN • REPRODUCTION PROHIBITED

(A) Sequence

Number the sentences from 1 to 6, in the correct order.

_____ New France becomes a British colony called British North America.

_____ Europeans explore Canada.

_____ Canada makes changes to the BNA Act.

_____ Only Aboriginal peoples live in Canada.

_____ Canada becomes independent and follows the rules in the BNA Act to govern itself.

_____ Parts of Canada become French colonies called New France.

Write the sentences in the correct order.

_____

_____

_____

_____

_____

_____

(B) Match

Draw a line to match the words to their meanings.

Constitution	**the same**
Act	**the laws of a government**
permission	**law**
Rights	**consent**
equal	**things we are entitled to**

THE CANADIAN CHARTER OF RIGHTS AND FREEDOMS

What Is the Charter of Rights and Freedoms?

The Charter of Rights and Freedoms is part of Canada's constitution. The constitution lists the most important rules of the government. The Charter lists important rights of Canadians.

Protection from Government

The Charter helps to make sure that government actions or laws respect our rights. It can protect us from anything the government does that violates our Charter rights. If you think one of your Charter rights has been violated, you can take the government to court.

Some of the rights in the Charter are language rights, legal rights and equality rights.

Other Human Rights Laws

Canada also has human rights laws. Each province has provincial human rights laws. These laws list our rights in the workplace, in hospitals, in schools, in public places, in finding housing and in buying goods and services. The human rights laws help make sure people treat each other fairly.

If you think your rights have been violated, you can complain to a human rights commission.

Understand What You Read

(A) Match

Here are some of the rights in the Charter of Rights and Freedoms. Draw a line to match the rights in the left column with the descriptions in the right column.

| Language Rights |
| Equality Rights |
| Legal Rights |
| Democratic Rights |
| Mobility Rights |

- right to vote
- right to join in political activities

- right to enter and leave Canada
- right to move to any province

- right to speak with the federal government in French or English
- right to speak with the provincial government of New Brunswick in French or English

- right to life
- right not to be unreasonably searched or taken away
- right not to get cruel or unusual punishment
- right to retain a lawyer

- right to be treated and protected equally by the law

(B) Answer the Questions

1. What does the Constitution Act list?

_____

2. What does the Charter of Rights and Freedoms list?

_____

3. What can you do if you think a government law violates one of your Charter rights?

_____

4. List four places where provincial human rights laws protect us.

_____

CELEBRATING OUR HISTORY:
VICTORIA DAY

Queen Elizabeth II

Canadians remember and celebrate their history every year.

Victoria Day

Canadians remember that Canada was a British colony. Every year Canadians celebrate Queen Victoria's birthday. She was born on May 24, 1819. She was the Queen of England when Canada became independent in 1867.

Every year, the third Monday in May is a holiday. We call this holiday Victoria Day.

The Queen Today

Today, the Queen of England is Queen Elizabeth II. Canada remembers and respects its history as a British colony. Canada has been an independent country since 1867, but Canada chooses to keep the Queen of England as its Head of State.

The Queen's picture is on all of our coins, some of our stamps and on our $20 bill.

Understand What You Read

(A) Circle the Correct Answer

1. The Queen's picture is on all of Canada's
   a) bills.
   b) coins.

2. In 1867, the Queen of England was
   a) Queen Elizabeth II.
   b) Queen Victoria.

3. Victoria Day celebrates Queen Victoria's
   a) birthday.
   b) marriage.

4. Today, the Queen's name is Queen
   a) Victoria.
   b) Elizabeth II.

5. The Queen's picture is on Canada's
   a) $20 bill.
   b) $10 bill.

6. Victoria Day is on the third Monday in
   a) July.
   b) May.

(B) Discuss

Some people think the Queen should not have a role in Canada. They think the monarchy is old-fashioned.

Others want the Queen to remain as Canada's head of state. They say the Queen is part of Canada's history. They think Canada should stay connected to the Queen.

What do you think? Why?

CELEBRATING OUR HISTORY:
CANADA DAY

On July 1, 1867, Canada became independent and started to govern itself. Every year, Canada celebrates its independence.

Canada Day

Every year, July 1 is a holiday. This holiday is called Canada Day. On Canada Day, we celebrate the day Canada became independent. Canada Day is also called Canada's birthday.

Canada's First Prime Minister

Canada's first prime minister was Sir John A. Macdonald. His picture is on our $10 bill. He became prime minister in 1867.

Canada also honours other past prime ministers. Sir Wilfrid Laurier is on our $5 bill. He became prime minister in 1896. Sir Robert Borden is on our $100 bill. He became prime minister in 1911. William Lyon Mackenzie King is on our $50 bill. He became prime minister in 1921.

Understand What You Read

(A) Answer the Questions

1. Complete the chart.

Bill	Prime Minister	Year He First Became Prime Minister
$5 bill		
$10 bill		
$50 bill		
$100 bill		

2. Who was Canada's first prime minister? _____

3. When is Canada Day? _____

4. When did Canada become independent? _____

5. Who governed Canada before independence? _____

6. How old is Canada today? _____

7. Who is pictured on our $20 bill? _____

8. Who is the prime minister today? _____

(B) Discuss

1. Do you celebrate Canada Day? How?

2. Does your country of origin celebrate its independence? How?

CELEBRATING OUR HISTORY:
ABORIGINAL PEOPLES

Every year, there is a special day to celebrate and appreciate Canada's Aboriginal peoples. It is called National Aboriginal Day. It is on June 21.

Why is National Aboriginal Day on June 21?

For many Aboriginal groups, June 21 is an important day. It is the first day of a new season. It is the first day of summer. June 21 is also the summer solstice.

What Is the Summer Solstice?

The summer solstice has more daylight hours than any other day of the year. It is the longest day of the year. Usually, June 21 is the summer solstice.

In Toronto, Ontario, there are about 15 and a half hours of daylight on June 21. In December, there are only about 9 hours of sunlight.

In the far north of Canada there are 24 hours of sunlight in June. Because of this, the land in the far north of Canada is sometimes called the **Land of the Midnight Sun**.

Understand What You Read

(A) Answer the Questions

1. When is National Aboriginal Day?

   _____

2. What is the summer solstice?

   _____

3. Why is the far north sometimes called the **Land of the Midnight Sun**?

   _____

4. Does your country of origin celebrate the change of seasons? How?

   _____

GLOSSARY
THE HISTORY

Aboriginal peoples:	The first people to live in a country
Band:	A group of North American Indians who share the same customs
BNA Act:	The British North American Act; a law signed by the British government in 1867 that explained how Canada would govern itself
British North America:	The land in North America that belonged to Britain (from 1763 to 1867)
Canada Day:	A holiday on July 1 celebrating Canada's birthday
Charter of Rights and Freedoms:	Part of Canada's constitution; lists basic rights of Canadians
Colony:	Land a country owns that is far away
Confederation:	The union of different areas of land
Constitution Act:	The new name for the BNA Act in 1982
Eskimo:	Another name for the Inuit
First Nations:	Another name for the North American Indians
Fur trade:	The trade in beaver furs between Aboriginal peoples and Europeans
Independent:	Self-governing
Inuit:	A group of Aboriginal people who live in the North of Canada
Inuktitut:	The language of the Inuit
Kanata:	A word that means *village* in an Aboriginal language
Loyalists:	People who moved from the United States to Canada after the United States became independent
Métis:	People descended from North American Indians and Europeans
National Aboriginal Day:	On June 21; celebrates Aboriginal peoples
New France:	French colonies in what is now Canada
North American Indians:	A group of Aboriginal peoples
Reserves:	Areas of land saved for North American Indians
Settlers:	People who move to a new undeveloped land to live
The thirteen colonies:	British colonies in parts of what is now the United States
Victoria Day:	A holiday in May that celebrates Queen Victoria's birthday

PART 4
THE GOVERNMENT

Canada's Government

Get Ready to Learn		**108**
Unit 1	The Levels of Government	**109**
Unit 2	Government Spending	**112**
Unit 3	Canada Is a Democracy	**114**
Unit 4	Who Can Vote?	**117**

The Federal Government

Unit 5	Ridings	**120**
Unit 6	Political Parties	**124**
Unit 7	Members of Parliament	**126**
Unit 8	House of Commons	**128**
Unit 9	Government Spending	**130**
Unit 10	The Prime Minister	**132**
Unit 11	Prime Ministers of Canada	**136**
Unit 12	The Cabinet	**138**
Unit 13	The Senate	**141**
Unit 14	The Governor General	**143**
Unit 15	Summary	**145**

The Provincial Government

Unit 16	Ridings	**146**
Unit 17	Members of Provincial Legislature	**148**
Unit 18	Government Spending	**151**
Unit 19	Political Parties	**152**
Unit 20	The Premier	**153**
Unit 21	The Cabinet	**156**
Unit 22	The Lieutenant Governor	**158**
Unit 23	Provincial Government: Summary	**160**
Unit 24	Provincial and Federal Government: Summary	**161**

The Municipal Government

Unit 25	The Municipal Government	**162**
Unit 26	Responsibilities	**164**
Unit 27	Members of Government	**166**
Unit 28	The Federal, Provincial and Municipal Government: Review	**168**
Glossary		**172**

TO LEARN ABOUT...

Canada's Government

In Units one to twenty-eight, you will learn about Canada's government.

Before you work on the units, try to answer these questions.

1. Have you ever voted in an election? Describe your experience.

2. Do you think it is important to vote? Why?

3. Can you name Canada's three levels of government?

4. Do you remember the year of the last election? Was it a federal, provincial or municipal election? What do you remember about it?

5. Think about each level of government. Write as many words as you can for each level of government, such as prime minister, premier and so on.

Federal Government	Provincial Government	Municipal Government
_____	_____	_____
_____	_____	_____
_____	_____	_____
_____	_____	_____

6. Do you want to learn more about Canada's government? What do you want to learn?

THE LEVELS OF GOVERNMENT

What Is a Government?

A government is a group of people who make decisions about how to run a country or an area of land. Canada has three levels of government.

The Federal Government

The federal government makes laws for all of Canada.

The Provincial or Territorial Governments

The provincial or territorial governments make laws for a province or territory.

The Municipal Government

The municipal government makes laws for a municipality. A municipality is a city, town, township or village.

A city

The Federal Government

The federal government is the government of Canada. The federal government makes decisions about things that affect all Canadians. It decides about issues like immigration, defence, health care and employment. The federal government holds its meetings in Ottawa, Canada's capital city.

Federal government symbol

The Provincial Government

Canada is a large country. People in different areas have different concerns. For example, fishing is important to people in Nova Scotia, but people in Saskatchewan care more about wheat farming. So each province and territory has its own government. It is called the **provincial** or **territorial** government.

Each provincial government makes decisions for its own province. Provincial governments decide about things like education, health care and highways. The provincial government holds its meetings in the capital city of the province.

The Municipal Government

There are hundreds of cities and towns in Canada. People in different cities have different concerns. So each city has its own government. It is called the municipal government.

Municipal governments make decisions for their own communities. They decide about things like policing, recycling, roads and snow removal.

Understand What You Read

(A) Fill in the Blanks

Write the correct level of government under each map.

| Provincial Government • Municipal Government • Federal Government |

A city

(B) Circle the Correct Answer

1. The federal government makes decisions for

    a) only one province.
    b) the whole country.
    c) only one city.

2. Each provincial government makes decisions for

    a) only one province.
    b) every province.
    c) only one city.

3. Canada has

    a) one federal government.
    b) three federal governments.
    c) ten federal governments.

4. Canada has

    a) three provincial governments.
    b) ten provincial governments.
    c) one provincial government.

5. Canada has

    a) one territorial government.
    b) ten territorial governments.
    c) three territorial governments.

GOVERNMENT SPENDING

The government gets its money from many sources. Most of its money comes from income taxes and consumption taxes. Consumption taxes are taxes on the things we buy.

What Does the Government Do with Its Money?

The government spends its money on many different programs and services for Canadians. Each level of government spends its money in different ways.

The chart below shows how Canada's federal government, provincial and territorial governments and municipal governments combined spent each dollar in the 2008/2009 fiscal year (from April 1, 2008 to March 31, 2009).

Total Government Spending (2008/2009) For all three levels of government	
For Each Government Dollar:	
Social services	30¢
Health	19¢
Education	15¢
Protection of people and property	8¢
Interest on debt	7¢
Transportation and communications	5¢
General government services	4¢
Resource conservation and industrial development	3¢
Environment	3¢
Recreation and culture	3¢
Foreign affairs and international assistance	1¢
Housing	1¢
Other spending and surplus	1¢
	$1.00

Source: Adapted from the Statistics Canada website, Jan. 2010,
http://www40.statcan.gc.ca/101/cst01/govt48b-eng.htm.

Understand What You Read

(A) Answer the Questions

1. Where does most of Canada's government money come from?

_____

2. What are consumption taxes?

_____

3. In 2008/2009, almost 65¢ of each government dollar was spent on three areas. Name the areas.

_____

4. In 2008/2009, how much of each government dollar was spent on interest for government debts?

_____

(B) Discuss in Groups

1. Social services include programs that help people with low incomes live better lives. Social services also include programs for senior citizens.

Brainstorm with your group. List as many social services as you can think of.

_____   _____

_____   _____

_____   _____

2. Government health spending includes paying for what we need to make sure all Canadians can get medical care when they need it.

Brainstorm with your group. Make a list of government health costs.

_____   _____

_____   _____

_____   _____

CANADA IS A DEMOCRACY

Canada is a democracy. That means that Canadians decide who will govern Canada.

What Is a Government?

Every few years, Canadians choose a group of people to govern Canada and its provinces and cities. This group of people is our government. Our government works for all Canadians.

Who Are the Members of a Government?

The members of a government are people who help make decisions about how to run a country, province or municipality. During an election, a person who wants to be elected as a government member is called a **candidate**.

How Do We Choose Members of a Government?

Canada's government changes every few years. Before the government changes, there is an **election**. During an election, we choose people to govern Canada. We choose them by voting for them on voting day. The people we choose form our government.

The Election Campaign

Before voting day, there is an election campaign. Many things happen during an election campaign. Candidates try to convince you to vote for them. They make speeches. They put their names on signs. They put pamphlets in your mailbox. Sometimes they come to your home to greet you personally. We listen to the candidates. We try to decide whose ideas we like. The campaign lasts about a month.

There are federal elections, provincial and territorial elections and municipal elections. These elections usually happen at different times.

Understand What You Read

(A) Match

Write the correct letters on the lines to match the words with their meanings.

_____ Democracy   a) A group of people who make decisions about a country

_____ Election   b) A brochure or leaflet

_____ Candidate   c) The people decide who will govern their country

_____ Pamphlet   d) A person who wants to be elected as a politician

_____ Election campaign   e) The days before voting day when candidates try to convince Canadians to vote for them

_____ Government   f) A time when we choose people to govern Canada

_____ Vote   g) Choose

(B) Answer the Questions

1. What is an election campaign?

_____

2. About how long does an election campaign last?

_____

3. When does an election campaign happen?

_____

4. List three things that happen during an election campaign.

_____

5. What happens after the election campaign?

_____

C) Fill in the Blanks

provincial · people · voting · voting day · years
democracy · federal · different · municipal · election
candidate · election campaign · government

1. Canada is a _____.

2. A democracy means that the _____ decide who will
   govern their country.

3. Canadians choose politicians by _____ for them.

4. Canadians vote for politicians when there is an _____.

5. Federal, provincial and municipal elections happen at _____
   _____ times.

6. Canada's governments change every few _____.

7. The day we vote is called _____.

8. The _____ happens before voting day.

9. The _____ changes after an election.

10. A _____ is someone who wants to get elected as a
    government member.

11. The government of Canada is the _____ government.

12. The government of a province is the _____ government.

13. The government of a city is the _____ government.

D) Discuss

1. Has a candidate ever come to your door? What happened?

2. Describe the election process in your country of origin.

3. Would you want to be a candidate in an election? Why or why not?

Who Can Vote in Canada's Elections?

You can vote if you are an adult and a Canadian citizen. An adult means you are eighteen years old or older.

A Canadian citizen means:

- you were born in Canada or
- you became a Canadian citizen

How Do You Vote?

If you can vote, your name should be on the **voters' list**. The voters' list is a list of Canadians who are allowed to vote.

If your name is on the voters' list, you will get a card in the mail. It will arrive before voting day. The card tells you where to vote on voting day.

On voting day, you go to the address written on the card. There you get a **ballot**. A ballot is a piece of paper with the names of candidates on it. You vote by putting a mark beside the name of the candidate you like.

After you vote, you put your ballot in a ballot box. At the end of voting day, someone counts the votes. The candidate with the most votes gets elected.

Does Everyone Vote?

Only adult Canadian citizens can vote. But not all adult Canadian citizens vote. Some people choose not to vote. After every election, we find out the **voter turnout**.

The voter turnout tells us the percentage of eligible voters who voted. A high voter turnout means that many Canadians voted.

Voter Turnout in Canada's Federal Elections	
Election Year	**Percent of Eligible Voters**
1988	75%
1993	70%
1997	67%
2000	61%
2004	61%
2006	65%
2008	59%

Source: Elections Canada.

Understand What You Read

(A) Complete the Crossword

DOWN ↓

1. We vote during an ___.
2. Only Canadian ___ can vote.
3. After you vote, you put your ballot in the ___.
4. The percentage of adult Canadian citizens who voted is the ___.
5. A list of eligible voters is a ___.
6. People 18 and over are ___.

ACROSS →

7. A ___ voter turnout is when many Canadians vote in an election.
8. You ___ on a ballot.
9. A ___ is someone who wants to be a politician.
10. A ___ voter turnout is when not many Canadians vote in an election.
11. If you were born in ___ you are a Canadian citizen.
12. You vote on a ___.

ballot box • vote • ballot • Canada • election • voters' list
adults • citizens • low • candidate • voter turnout • high

(B) Discuss

1. Why do you think some Canadians don't vote?

2. How do you think Canada can increase its voter turnout?

C Sequence

Number the sentences from one to six.

_____ You get a ballot.

_____ You put your ballot in the ballot box.

_____ You get a card in the mail. It tells you where to vote.

_____ You vote by putting a mark beside the name of a candidate listed on the ballot.

_____ It is voting day. You go to the address written on your card.

_____ Voting day is over. Someone counts the votes.

Write the sentences in order.

1. _____

2. _____

3. _____

4. _____

5. _____

6. _____

D Match

Write the correct letter on the lines to match the words with their meanings.

_____ Voters' list   a) A box for completed ballots

_____ Ballot   b) A person who is trying to get elected as
                                    a government member

_____ Ballot box   c) A person 18 years or older

_____ Candidate   d) A piece of paper with the names of
                                    candidates running for election

_____ Adult   e) A list of eligible voters

THE FEDERAL GOVERNMENT: RIDINGS

What Is a Riding?

Canada is divided into voting areas. Each area of land has about the same number of people in it. The areas are called **ridings**. Ridings are also called electoral districts or constituencies. Everyone in Canada lives in a riding. We only vote in our own riding.

How Many Ridings Are There?

There are 308 federal ridings in Canada. During an election, the people in each riding elect one **Member of Parliament** to represent them. The Parliament of Canada includes all the politicians we elect in a federal election. In the federal election of 2008, 308 Members of Parliament got elected.

There are more people in some provinces than other provinces. Ontario has more people than any other province. So Ontario is divided into more ridings than the other provinces. Because of this, there are more politicians from Ontario than from the other provinces.

Federal Ridings Provinces and Territories, (as of 2010)		
Province/Territory	Ridings	Elected Politicians
British Columbia	36	36
Alberta	28	28
Saskatchewan	14	14
Manitoba	14	14
Ontario	106	106
Quebec	75	75
New Brunswick	10	10
Nova Scotia	11	11
Prince Edward Island	4	4
Newfoundland and Labrador	7	7
Yukon Territory	1	1
Northwest Territories	1	1
Nunavut	1	1
CANADA	308	308

Ridings Change Every Ten Years

Every ten years, the number of ridings in Canada changes. This is done to reflect increases in Canada's population.

For example, in the 1949 federal election there were only 262 ridings. Most of the growth in population since then has taken place in Ontario, Alberta and British Columbia, so that's where most of the newer ridings have been created.

No Province Can Lose Ridings

In 1985, Canada passed a law that said no province can lose ridings, even if its population decreases or is growing slower than other provinces.

Understand What You Read

(A) **Circle the Correct Answer**

1. Canada has _____ federal government(s).
   a) one
   b) ten
   c) three

2. Canada (as of 2010) is divided into _____ federal ridings.
   a) 10
   b) 308
   c) 103

3. In 1949, Canada had _____ ridings.
   a) 106
   b) 262
   c) 308

4. Two other names for a riding are _____.
   a) a constituency and a politician
   b) an electoral district and a riding
   c) an electoral district and a constituency

5. Each riding _____.
   a) is the same size
   b) has about the same number of people
   c) is the same size and has the same number of people

6. You can vote _____.
   a) in every riding
   b) in any riding in your province
   c) only in the riding you live in

7. Each riding elects _____ Member(s) of Parliament.
   a) 308
   b) one
   c) 10

8. If a province has a high population, it has _____.
   a) more ridings than other provinces.
   b) fewer ridings than other provinces.

9. If a province's population decreases, _____.
   a) its number of ridings stay the same
   b) its number of ridings increase
   c) its number of ridings decrease

B **Answer the Questions**

1. On the map below, write the number of federal ridings in each province and territory. Saskatchewan is filled in for you.

2. How many ridings are in your province?

3. How many politicians get elected to Parliament from your province?

4. How many politicians get elected to Parliament in total?

5. How often do the number of ridings change?

6. Why do the number of ridings change?

7. In which provinces have most of the newer ridings been created?

C Answer the Questions

Here is an imaginary country called Glat. Imagine there are one hundred people in Glat.

1. Draw boundaries on the map to divide Glat into ten ridings.

   Each riding should have ten people in it. One riding is drawn for you.

GLAT

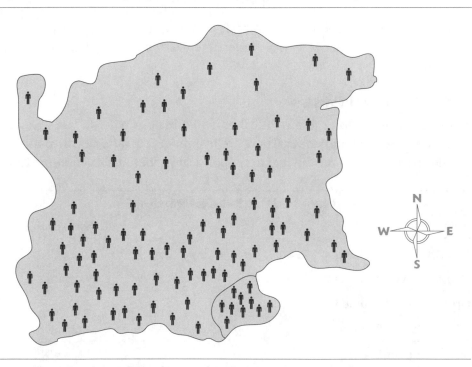

2. Is each riding the same size?   _____

3. Does each riding have the same number of people in it?   _____

4. The people in each riding elect one politician.
   How many politicians form the government of Glat?   _____

5. If everyone moves to the northern part of Glat,
      a) will every riding still have ten people in it?   _____

      b) will we need to change the boundaries of the ridings?   _____

THE FEDERAL GOVERNMENT: POLITICAL PARTIES

What Is a Political Party?

A political party is a group of people who have similar ideas about how to run the country. Each political party has a leader.

There are federal political parties and provincial political parties. Usually, there are no municipal political parties.

Sometimes provincial parties and federal parties have the same name. For example, there is a federal Liberal Party, and each province also has a provincial Liberal Party. The federal Liberal Party has one leader, and each provincial Liberal Party has a different leader.

Federal Political Parties

Most politicians belong to a political party. Politicians who do not belong to a political party are called **independents**. There are five main federal political parties and other smaller parties. Here are the five main political parties and their short forms:

Five Main Federal Political Parties	
Political Party	**Short Form**
Bloc Québécois	BQ
Conservative Party of Canada	Conservative
Green Party of Canada	Green
Liberal Party of Canada	Liberal
New Democratic Party	NDP

Each political party has a party symbol.

During an election, candidates put their names on party signs. Each political party can have only one candidate in each riding.

Understand What You Read

(A) Answer the Questions

1. What is a political party?

   _____

2. List four different federal political parties.

   _____

3. What is the short form for the Liberal Party of Canada?

   _____

4. Are federal and provincial political parties the same?

   _____

5. Do all politicians belong to a political party?

   _____

6. Which party is in power today?

   _____

(B) Fill in the Blanks

Write the names of the federal party leaders. You can find out the leaders' names by asking a friend, reading the newspaper, calling Elections Canada at 1-800-463-6868 or going to the Elections Canada website at www.elections.ca.

Federal Political Parties	
Political Party	**Party Leader**
Bloc Québécois	_____
Conservative Party of Canada	_____
Green Party of Canada	_____
Liberal Party of Canada	_____
New Democratic Party	_____

UNIT 7

THE FEDERAL GOVERNMENT: MEMBERS OF PARLIAMENT

During an election, we vote for one candidate from our riding. Some ridings have a candidate from each of the five main political parties. Sometimes there are candidates from other smaller political parties. Sometimes there are independent candidates, too.

A ballot lists all the candidates in a riding. It looks something like the sample on the right.

Canadians Elect MPs

After the election, someone counts the votes. In each riding, the candidate with the most votes wins the election. He or she becomes a **Member of Parliament**. This is a long name, so we shorten it to MP. The people in each of Canada's 308 ridings elect an MP this way.

The 308 elected MPs each have an office in their riding. Each MP also works and goes to meetings in Ottawa.

Ballot

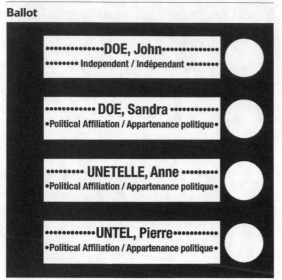

•••••••••••DOE, John•••••••••••
•••••••• Independent / Indépendant ••••••••

••••••••••• DOE, Sandra •••••••••••
•Political Affiliation / Appartenance politique•

•••••••• UNETELLE, Anne •••••••••
•Political Affiliation / Appartenance politique•

•••••••••••UNTEL, Pierre•••••••••••
•Political Affiliation / Appartenance politique•

Note: The above names are fictional.

Understand What You Read

(A) Answer the Questions

You can call the federal elections office at 1-800-463-6868 (or visit the website at www.elections.ca) to answer the questions below.

1. What is the name of your federal riding (or electoral district)?

_____

2. Who is the MP for your riding?

_____

3. What is the office address and phone number of your MP?

_____

B) Fill in the Blanks

> Parliament · one · MP · riding · ballot
> Ottawa · capital city · five · independent · 308

1. The short form for a Member of Parliament is an _____.

2. Canada's Parliament includes _____ MPs.

3. Every riding elects _____ MP.

4. A _____ lists all the candidates in a riding.

5. There are _____ main federal political parties.

6. An MP who does not belong to a political party is an _____.

7. An MP is a Member of _____.

8. Each MP has an office in his or her _____.

9. MPs have meetings in _____.

10. Ottawa is Canada's _____.

C) Answer the Questions

Look at the sample ballot on the previous page.

1. How many candidates want to be elected in this riding?

_____

2. Which candidate is an independent?

_____

3. We vote by putting a mark on the ballot. Where on the ballot do you think we make the mark?

_____

THE FEDERAL GOVERNMENT:
HOUSE OF COMMONS

Where Do MPs Have Meetings?

Members of Parliament (MPs) have meetings at the Parliament Buildings in Ottawa. They meet in the House of Commons. The first picture below is a picture of the Parliament Buildings.

What Is the House of Commons?

The House of Commons is a large room in the Parliament Buildings. In the House of Commons, there is one seat for each of the 308 MPs. The members of the House of Commons are the MPs.

What Do the MPs Do at These Meetings?

MPs talk about how to govern Canada. They talk about things that concern Canadians. They make laws for Canada. They decide how to spend government money.

Here is a picture of the House of Commons. It is inside the middle building of the Parliament Buildings. The middle building is called the Centre Block.

Understand What You Read

(A) Match

_____ House of Commons

_____ Parliament Buildings

_____ Ridings

_____ Electoral district

_____ Member of Parliament

_____ Ottawa

_____ Federal government

_____ Centre Block

a) Another word for a riding

b) MP

c) The middle building of the Parliament Buildings

d) Government buildings in Ottawa in which MPs meet

e) Areas of land with about the same number of people

f) The room in which MPs meet

g) Capital city of Canada

h) Government of Canada

(B) Answer the Questions

1. How many seats are in the House of Commons?

_____

2. Where is the House of Commons?

_____

3. In a federal election, we elect Members of Parliament. What is the short form of this title?

_____

4. What is the capital city of Canada?

_____

5. Who are the members of the House of Commons?

_____

(C) Discuss

Have you ever visited Ottawa? Did you see the Parliament Buildings? Describe them.

THE FEDERAL GOVERNMENT: GOVERNMENT SPENDING

Where Does the Federal Government Get Its Money?

The federal government gets its money from many sources. Most of its money comes from income taxes and consumption taxes.

Consumption taxes include tax on the things we buy, gasoline tax, tobacco tax and tax on alcohol. Income tax is the tax we pay on money we earn from a job.

How Does the Federal Government Spend Its Money?

The federal government spends its money on many services and programs for Canadians.

Every year, the government announces a budget. The budget tells us how much money the government plans to spend on each service and program.

For example, in the 2008/2009 fiscal year, the federal government spent $242 billion. Most of the money (80 percent) was spent on social services, health, interest on the federal government debt, payments to provinces and territories and programs that protect people.

The payments to provinces and territories help the provinces and territories pay for health, education and other programs

Federal Government Spending (2008/2009)	
80¢ of Each Dollar Was Spent On:	
Social services	37¢
Payments to provinces and territories	12¢
Protection of people and property	12¢
Health	11¢
Interest on the federal debt	8¢

Source: Adapted from the Statistics Canada website, Jan. 2010, http://www40.statcan.gc.ca/101/cst01/govt49b-eng.htm.

Understand What You Read

A Answer the Questions

1. Name two ways the federal government gets its money.

   _____

2. How often does the government announce a budget?

   _____

3. What does the budget tell us?

   _____

4. In the 2008/2009 fiscal year, how much did the federal government spend?

   _____

5. On what five things did the government spend 80 percent of its money?

   _____

6. In 2008/2009, how much of every dollar was spent on federal debt charges?

   _____

B Discuss in Groups

1. Canada's government has a debt. Every year, the government spends a lot of money on interest payments on its debt.

   What are some advantages and disadvantages to paying off the debt more quickly?

Advantages	Disadvantages
_____	_____
_____	_____
_____	_____

2. In Canada, we pay a 5 percent sales tax on most of the goods and services we buy. For many things, we also pay a provincial sales tax. These taxes help pay for government programs and services.

   Do you think our sales taxes are too high, too low or just right? Why?

THE FEDERAL GOVERNMENT: THE PRIME MINISTER

Who Is the Prime Minister?

The prime minister is the leader of the federal government.

How Does the Prime Minister Get His or Her Job?

On voting day the people in each riding elect one Member of Parliament (MP). After all the ridings have elected an MP, we find out how many MPs belong to each political party.

The political party with the most elected MPs becomes the party in power and forms the government. The leader of that political party becomes the prime minister. The prime minister is an MP, too.

The chart below shows how Canadians voted in the 2006 and 2008 federal elections. It shows how many MPs belonged to each party.

The 2008 Election

Canadians elected more MPs from the Conservative Party than from any other party. The Conservative Party remained the party in power. The leader of the Conservative Party, Stephen Harper, remained the prime minister.

How Long Does a Party Stay in Power?

The prime minister can call another election any time, but it must be within five years of the last election.

MPs Elected in the 2006 and 2008 Federal Election		
	2006	**2008**
Conservative Party of Canada	124	143
Liberal Party of Canada	103	77
Bloc Québécois	51	49
New Democratic Party	29	37
Green Party of Canada	0	0
Other	1	2
TOTAL MPs	**308**	**308**

Understand What You Read

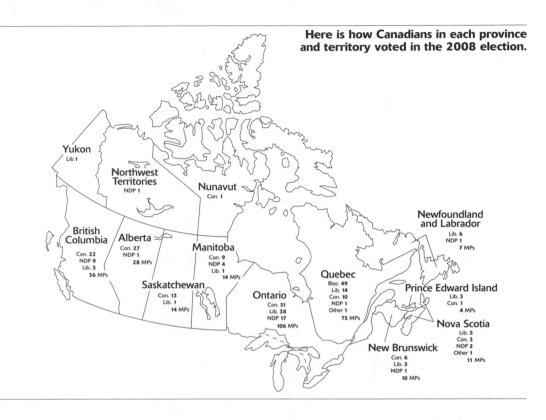

Here is how Canadians in each province and territory voted in the 2008 election.

Yukon
Lib.1

Northwest Territories
NDP 1

Nunavut
Con. 1

British Columbia
Con. 22
NDP 9
Lib. 5
36 MPs

Alberta
Con. 27
NDP 1
28 MPs

Manitoba
Con. 9
NDP 4
Lib. 1
14 MPs

Saskatchewan
Con. 13
Lib. 1
14 MPs

Ontario
Con. 51
Lib. 38
NDP 17
106 MPs

Quebec
Bloc: 49
Lib. 14
Con. 10
NDP 1
Other 1
75 MPs

Newfoundland and Labrador
Lib. 6
NDP 1
7 MPs

Prince Edward Island
Lib. 3
Con. 1
4 MPs

Nova Scotia
Lib. 5
Con. 3
NDP 2
Other 1
11 MPs

New Brunswick
Con. 6
Lib. 3
NDP 1
10 MPs

(A) Fill in the Blanks

Look at the map. Next to each province or territory, write the number of MPs elected from each party on the chart. British Columbia has been filled in.

Number of MPs elected in 2008							
	Conservative	Liberal	*Bloc Québécois	NDP	Other		Total
British Columbia	22	5		9		=	36
Alberta						=	28
Saskatchewan						=	14
Manitoba						=	14
Ontario						=	106
Quebec						=	75
New Brunswick						=	10
Nova Scotia						=	11
Prince Edward Island						=	4
Newfoundland and Labrador						=	7
Yukon						=	1
Northwest Territories						=	1
Nunavut						=	1
Total MPs	**143**	**77**	**49**	**37**	**2**	**=**	**308**

* The Bloc Québécois only has MPs from Quebec. It does not have candidates in any other province during elections.

B) Answer the Questions

1. How many MPs were elected in the 2008 election?

_____

2. Did all the MPs belong to a political party?

_____

3. Which party had the most elected MPs in the 2008 election?

_____

4. Which party became the party in power in the 2008 election?

_____

5. Which party became the party in power in the 2006 election?

_____

6. Who was the leader of the Conservative Party of Canada in 2008?

_____

7. Who became the prime minister in the 2008 election?

_____

8. Compare the 2006 and the 2008 election results. Which political parties became more popular between 2006 and 2008?

_____

9. Which political parties became less popular between 2006 and 2008?

_____

C) Fill in the Blanks

Look at the chart you filled in on the previous page. On the lines below, fill in the names of the correct provinces.

1. In which province did all Bloc Québécois MPs get elected?

_____

2. In which two provinces did most Liberal Party MPs get elected?

_____ and _____

3. Which province's voters did not elect any MPs from the Liberal Party?

_____

(D) Circle True or False

1. On voting day we vote for a prime minister.   T   F

2. On voting day we vote for a Member of Parliament.   T   F

3. The prime minister can call an election after six years.   T   F

4. The prime minister is the leader of the federal government.   T   F

5. The prime minister is the leader of the party in power.   T   F

6. In the 2008 election, the Liberal Party became the party in power.   T   F

(E) Answer the Questions

1. Write the names of the party leaders. To find the correct information, you can ask a friend, read the newspaper, call Elections Canada at 1-800-463-6868 or access the Elections Canada website at www.elections.ca.

Federal Party Leaders		
Political Party	Party Leader, (as of Jan. 2010)	Party Leader Today
Bloc Québécois	Gilles Duceppe	
Conservative Party of Canada	Stephen Harper	
Green Party of Canada	Elizabeth May	
Liberal Party of Canada	Michael Ignatieff	
New Democratic Party	Jack Layton	

2. Which (if any) political parties have different leaders today than they did in January 2010?

_____

3. Which party is in power today?

_____

4. Who is the prime minister today?

_____

THE FEDERAL GOVERNMENT:
PRIME MINISTERS OF CANADA

Canadian Prime Ministers		
Prime Minister	**Party**	**Years in power**
Sir John A. Macdonald	Conservative	1867 – 1873
Alexander Mackenzie	Liberal	1873 – 1878
*Sir John A. Macdonald	Conservative	1878 – 1891
Sir John Joseph Caldwell Abbott	Conservative	1891 – 1892
Sir John Sparrow David Thompson	Conservative	1892 – 1894
Sir Mackenzie Bowell	Conservative	1894 – 1896
Sir Charles Tupper	Conservative	1896
Sir Wilfrid Laurier	Liberal	1896 – 1911
Sir Robert Laird Borden	Conservative	1911 – 1920
Arthur Meighen	Conservative	1920 – 1921
William Lyon Mackenzie King	Liberal	1921 – 1926
*Arthur Meighen	Conservative	1926
*William Lyon Mackenzie King	Liberal	1926 – 1930
Richard Bedford Bennett	Conservative	1930 – 1935
*William Lyon Mackenzie King	Liberal	1935 – 1948
Louis Stephen St. Laurent	Liberal	1948 – 1957
John George Diefenbaker	Progressive Conservative	1957 – 1963
Lester Bowles Pearson	Liberal	1963 – 1968
Pierre Elliot Trudeau	Liberal	1968 – 1979
Charles Joseph Clark	Progressive Conservative	1979 – 1980
*Pierre Elliot Trudeau	Liberal	1980 – 1984
John Napier Turner	Liberal	1984
Martin Brian Mulroney	Progressive Conservative	1984 – 1993
Kim Campbell	Progressive Conservative	1993
Jean Chrétien	Liberal	1993 – 2003
Paul Martin	Liberal	2003 – 2006
Stephen Harper	Conservative	2006 –

Note: The stars mean it is NOT the first time a prime minister's name is on the list.

Understand What You Read

(A) Answer the Questions

  1. Who was Canada's first prime minister?

_____

  2. How many different prime ministers has Canada had?

_____

  3. Has Canada ever had a prime minister who belonged to the New Democratic Party?

_____

  4. Who was prime minister of Canada during World War I (1914 – 1918)?

_____

  5. Canada has had one female prime minister. What was her name and when was she prime minister?

_____

  6. William Lyon Mackenzie King was prime minister for the longest time. List the years in which he was prime minister.

_____

  7. Which four prime ministers are on Canada's $5, $10, $50 and $100 bills?

_____

  8. Who is the prime minister today?

_____

  9. How many years has he or she been prime minister?

_____

  10. What political party does the prime minister belong to?

_____

(B) Discuss

Do you have a favourite political leader from your country of origin? Why is this leader your favourite?

THE FEDERAL GOVERNMENT: THE CABINET

The prime minister is the leader of the federal government. The prime minister chooses some Members of Parliament (MPs) to give him or her advice and to help form government policies. The MPs the prime minister chooses are called **cabinet ministers**. They are almost always the same political party as the prime minister.

What Do Cabinet Ministers Do?

Each cabinet minister advises the prime minister on a ministry. A ministry is a part of the government. There are usually 20 to 35 ministries. Here are four:

Citizenship, Immigration and Multiculturalism • Health
Finance • Foreign Affairs

What Is the Cabinet?

The prime minister and the cabinet ministers are the Cabinet.

What Does the Cabinet Do?

The Cabinet discusses how to spend government money. The Cabinet also forms policies for Canada and ideas for new laws.

A law is a rule everyone has to follow. When Cabinet members agree on an idea for a new law, they write it down. It is called a bill. Bills can be about how to tax Canadians, how to spend government money or many other things.

This was the 2009 federal Cabinet of Prime Minister Stephen Harper. At that time, there were 38 Cabinet members.

The Cabinet presents the bill to the rest of the MPs in the House of Commons. The MPs discuss the bill. Then they vote on the bill.

Understand What You Read

(A) Answer the Questions

Write the correct letter on the lines to match the words with their meanings.

_____ MP   a) Chosen by the prime minister

_____ PM   b) Includes all the Members of Parliament

_____ Cabinet   c) A part of the government

_____ Cabinet ministers   d) Member of Parliament

_____ Ministry   e) The prime minister and the cabinet ministers

_____ House of Commons   f) The prime minister

(B) Circle the Correct Answer

1. Canadians elect
   a) Members of Parliament.
   b) the Cabinet.
   c) cabinet ministers.

2. The prime minister chooses some MPs to be
   a) Members of Parliament.
   b) politicians.
   c) cabinet ministers.

3. The prime minister and the cabinet ministers are
   a) the House of Commons.
   b) the Cabinet.
   c) the government.

4. A bill is an idea for a new
   a) law.
   b) prime minister.
   c) Member of Parliament.

5. Parliament includes 308
   a) Members of Parliament.
   b) prime ministers.
   c) cabinet ministers.

(C) Complete the Crossword

ACROSS →

1. The cabinet ministers and the prime minister are the ___.
2. ___ elect MPs.
3. A rule all Canadians must follow
4. Before a bill becomes a law, MPs ___ on it.
5. The short form for prime minister
6. A ministry: Ministry of ___
7. A political party: Progressive ___
8. A political party: ___ Québécois
9. The leader of the government

DOWN ↓

10. A ___ gives advice to the prime minister about a ministry.
11. A ___ is an idea for a new law.
12. Canada's capital city
13. MPs meet in the ___ Buildings.
14. A ___ is a part of government.
15. Members of Parliament are members of the ___.
16. A political party: ___ Party of Canada
17. A political party: ___ ___ Party
18. Short for Member of Parliament

Word List

ministry	MP	Cabinet	law	Finance	Bloc
New Democratic	Ottawa	cabinet minister	bill	PM	
prime minister	Canadians	Liberal	House of Commons		
Conservative	vote	Parliament			

THE FEDERAL GOVERNMENT: THE SENATE

There are three parts to Canada's Parliament: the Queen, the House of Commons and the Senate.

The House of Commons is made up of the 308 Members of Parliament (MPs) we elected. The prime minister and cabinet ministers are also MPs.

What Is the Senate?

The Senate is made up of a group of people called senators. The Senate meets in the Parliament Buildings. There are 105 senators in the Senate today. The Senate's main job is to examine and vote on bills.

The prime minister chooses senators from all over Canada. They can keep their jobs until they are 75, even if the government changes.

Here is a picture of the Senate.

The Senate is in the Parliament Buildings in Ottawa.

The Senate looks like the House of Commons, but it is smaller.

How Does a Bill Become a Law?

First, the Cabinet presents a bill to the House of Commons. The MPs in the House of Commons listen to the bill. They discuss it. Sometimes they change it. Then they vote on the bill. If most of the MPs vote for the bill, it goes to the Senate.

The Senate listens to the bill. Senators discuss the bill. Then they vote on the bill. If the Senate votes for the bill, the Governor General signs the bill. Then it becomes a law for Canada. The Governor General represents the Queen.

Understand What You Read

A **Circle the Correct Answer**

1. The three parts of Parliament are the Queen,
   a) the Senate and the Cabinet.
   b) the House of Commons and the Senate.
   c) the Senate and the Cabinet.

2. The Senate is made up of
   a) 105 senators.
   b) 308 Members of Parliament.

3. The House of Commons is made up of
   a) 105 senators.
   b) 308 Members of Parliament.
   c) senators and Members of Parliament.

4. The prime minister chooses
   a) senators.
   b) Members of Parliament.

5. A senator is a
   a) cabinet minister.
   b) Member of Parliament.
   c) member of the Senate.

6. The Senate votes on a bill
   a) before the House of Commons has voted for it.
   b) after the House of Commons has voted for it.

B **Answer the Questions**

1. Where does the Senate meet?

   _____

2. How long can senators keep their jobs?

   _____

3. How many senators are in the Senate?

   _____

4. What happens to a bill after the Senate votes for it?

   _____

THE FEDERAL GOVERNMENT: THE GOVERNOR GENERAL

The prime minister is the leader of our government. Canada also has a Head of State. Canada's Head of State symbolizes Canada's connection to Britain.

The Queen of England, Queen Elizabeth II, is Canada's Head of State. The Queen does not live or work in Canada. So someone who lives in Canada does her job. This person is the Governor General.

Who Is the Governor General?

Today, our Governor General is Michaëlle Jean.

What Does the Governor General Do?

The Governor General's main job is to sign bills. When the Governor General signs a bill, the bill becomes a law for Canadians. Canadian politicians make our laws and make decisions about Canada. But the laws and decisions are only legal after the Governor General signs them.

What Else Does the Governor General Do?

The Governor General introduces new governments. She travels all over Canada and listens to Canadians. She honours special Canadians with awards.

**This is Michaëlle Jean.
She is Canada's Governor General.**

Understand What You Read

(A) Sort

Number the sentences in the correct order. Then copy the sentences onto the
lines below.

How a Bill Becomes a Law

_____ The Senate votes on the bill.

_____ The Cabinet writes a bill.

_____ The Governor General signs the bill to make it a law.

_____ The House of Commons votes on the bill.

_____ The Cabinet presents the bill to the House of Commons.

1. _____

2. _____

3. _____

4. _____

5. _____

(B) Answer the Questions

1. Who is Canada's Head of State?

_____

2. Who does the Queen's job in Canada?

_____

3. Who is the Governor General today?

_____

4. List two things the Governor General does.

_____

THE FEDERAL GOVERNMENT: SUMMARY

Fill in the missing information.

You can call Elections Canada at 1-800-463-6868 or access the Elections Canada website at www.elections.ca to find the information.

Federal Government

Governor General: _____

Party in power: _____

Prime Minister: _____

Year of last election: _____

My federal riding: _____

My Member of Parliament: _____

My MP's address: _____

My MP's phone number: _____

My MP's e-mail address: _____

THE PROVINCIAL GOVERNMENT: RIDINGS

The federal government makes decisions and laws for all of Canada. But it doesn't make decisions about everything. The provinces and territories make some decisions and laws on their own.

Provincial Governments

A provincial government is the government of a province. A territorial government is the government of a territory. Provincial and territorial governments make decisions about things like health care, education and highways.

There are ten provincial governments and three territorial governments.

Each provincial government makes laws and decisions for its own province.

How Do We Elect Members of the Provincial Government?

Each province or territory has its own elections. These elections usually happen at different times than the federal elections.

Each province is divided into ridings. They are also called electoral districts. Each riding has about the same number of people in it.

On voting day, we vote for a candidate from the riding we live in. Then someone counts the votes in our riding. The candidate with the most votes becomes a member of the provincial legislature. The **legislature** is the group of people who can make laws for each province. Each riding in the province elects one politician to the provincial legislature.

For example, New Brunswick has 55 provincial ridings. So 55 politicians form New Brunswick's legislature. They have meetings in Fredericton, the capital city of New Brunswick.

Most members of the provincial legislature have an office in their riding. They also go to meetings in the capital city of the province.

Are Provincial Ridings the Same as Federal Ridings?

In most provinces, provincial ridings are different from federal ridings. We live in a federal riding that has one name, and a provincial riding that has another name. For example, New Brunswick has 55 provincial ridings, but only ten federal ridings.

In Ontario, provincial and federal ridings are almost the same. There are 106 federal ridings in Ontario, and 107 provincial ridings.

Understand What You Read

A Fill in the Blanks

Canada • different • candidate • ten • capital city
electoral district • three • province • ridings

1. There are _____ provincial governments in Canada.

2. There are _____ territorial governments in Canada.

3. The federal government makes laws for all of _____.

4. The provincial government makes laws for its own _____.

5. Each province is divided into _____.

6. Federal ridings and provincial ridings are usually _____.

7. The provincial government has meetings in the _____.

8. Another name for a riding is an _____.

9. Someone who wants to be elected to the legislature is a _____.

B Answer the Questions

1. How many provincial ridings does New Brunswick have? _____

2. How many politicians do the people in each riding elect? _____

3. How many politicians are in the New Brunswick legislature? _____

4. Can the New Brunswick government make a law for Alberta? _____

5. Can the federal government make a law for Alberta? _____

6. Does every province have its election on the same day? _____

THE PROVINCIAL GOVERNMENT: MEMBERS OF PROVINCIAL LEGISLATURE

What Are Members of Provincial Legislature Called?

The provincial **legislature** includes all the politicians we elect in a provincial election. In different provinces, the members of the legislature have different names.

In most provinces, the members of the legislature are called **Members of the Legislative Assembly**, or MLAs. Here is a list of the different names of the members of the provincial and territorial legislatures.

Members of Provincial Legislatures		
Province	**Member of the Legislature**	**Short Form**
Ontario	Member of Provincial Parliament	MPP
Quebec	Member of the National Assembly	MNA
Newfoundland and Labrador	Member of the House Assembly	MHA
All other provinces and territories	Member of the Legislative Assembly	MLA

What Does the Provincial Legislature Do?

The provincial legislature forms, discusses and debates new policies and laws for the province. The legislature also decides how much money to spend on different programs and services.

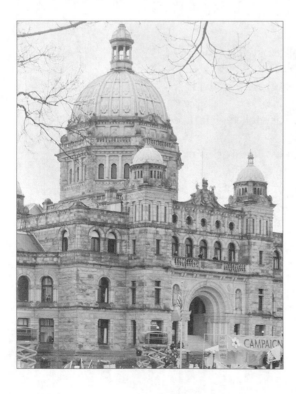

Where Do Members of the Provincial Legislature Have Meetings?

They have meetings in the capital city of their province or territory. Each province has a provincial government building.

Here is a picture of the government building in Victoria, British Columbia.

Understand What You Read

(A) Fill in the Blanks

Write the short form of each title.

1. Member of the House Assembly   _____

2. Member of the National Assembly   _____

3. Member of the Provincial Parliament   _____

4. Member of the Legislative Assembly   _____

5. Member of Parliament   _____

(B) Circle the Correct Answer

1. An _____ is a member of the federal Parliament.

   a) MPP
   b) MLA
   c) MP

2. An MPP is a member of the _____ legislature.

   a) Ontario
   b) Quebec
   c) Yukon

3. MNAs have meetings in the capital city of _____

   a) Nova Scotia
   b) Ontario
   c) Quebec

4. MPPs have meetings in _____.

   a) Toronto
   b) Victoria
   c) Ottawa

5. In most provinces, members of the provincial legislature are called _____.

   a) MPPs
   b) MLAs
   c) MNAs

(C) Fill in the Blanks

Write the city in which each provincial or territorial government has meetings.

British Columbia _____

Alberta _____

Saskatchewan _____

Manitoba _____

Ontario _____

Quebec _____

New Brunswick _____

Nova Scotia _____

Prince Edward Island _____

Newfoundland and Labrador _____

Yukon Territory _____

Northwest Territories _____

Nunavut _____

(D) Answer the Questions

You can find the answers by calling your provincial elections office. Look up Elections in the blue pages of your telephone book to find the phone number (The Ontario election office phone number is 1-800-677-8683. The website is www.electionsontario.ca).

1. What is the name of your provincial riding?

_____

2. Who is the MPP, MLS, MNA or MHA for your riding?

_____

3. What is his or her office address, e-mail address and phone number?

_____

THE PROVINCIAL GOVERNMENT: GOVERNMENT SPENDING

Where Do the Provincial Governments Get Money?

Provincial governments get their money from many sources. A provincial government gets most of its money from income taxes, consumption taxes and from the federal government.

How Do the Provincial Governments Spend Money?

The provincial governments spend money on many services and programs for people who live in the province. Most of the money goes to health, education and social services.

The chart below shows how the provinces and territories combined spent over 80 percent of their money.

For the Combined Provincial/Territorial Governments (2008/2009)	
81¢ of Each Dollar Was Spent On:	
Health	33¢
Education	23¢
Social services	18¢
Debt charges	7¢

Source: *Adapted from the Statistics Canada website, Jan. 2010, http://www40.statcan.gc.ca/l01/cst01/govt55a-eng.htm.*

The governments spent the remaining 19 percent of their money on protecting people and property, transportation, resource conservation, the environment, housing and other expenditures.

Understand What You Read

(A) Discuss

1. List three sources of income for the provincial governments.

   _____

2. Do you think the federal government gives each province and territory the same amount of money every year?

3. How do you think the federal government decides how much money to give each province and territory?

THE PROVINCIAL GOVERNMENT:
POLITICAL PARTIES

Most provincial politicians belong to a political party. Each political party has a leader. You can find out the leaders of the political parties in your province by calling your provincial elections office.

In the box below, write the names of the main political parties and party leaders for your province:

Provincial Political Parties
Provincial Elections Office Phone Number: _____

Political Party	Party Leader
_____	_____
_____	_____
_____	_____
_____	_____
_____	_____

For review, write the names of the main federal political parties and party leaders below:

Federal Political Parties
Federal Elections Office Phone Number: 1-800-463-6868

Political Party	Party Leader
Bloc Québécois	_____
Conservative Party of Canada	_____
Green Party of Canada	_____
Liberal Party of Canada	_____
New Democratic Party	_____

THE PROVINCIAL GOVERNMENT: THE PREMIER

Who Is the Premier?

The premier is the leader of the provincial government.

How Do We Elect the Premier?

On voting day, each riding in the province elects a member of the provincial legislature. After the election, we find out how many elected members belong to each party. The party with the most members becomes the party in power and forms the government. The leader of that party becomes the premier.

For example, here are the results of the Ontario election of 2007:

Ontario's 2007 Election Results	
Elections Ontario Website: www.elections.on.ca	
Political Party	**MPPs Elected**
Ontario Liberal Party	71
Progressive Conservative Party of Ontario	26
Ontario New Democratic Party	10
TOTAL Ontario MPPs	**107**

The Liberal Party of Ontario had more elected members of the legislature (called MPPs in Ontario) than the other parties. So the leader of the Liberal Party became the premier of Ontario. The Liberal Party became the party in power and formed Ontario's government.

How Long Will the Liberal Party Be in Power?

Elections in Ontario generally take place every four years. The next Ontario election is scheduled for October 6, 2011.

Understand What You Read

(A) Fill in the Blanks

| riding • four • provincial • party in power |
| one • federal • premier |

1. On voting day, we vote for a candidate from our _____.

2. Each riding in the province elects _____ member of the provincial legislature.

3. The party with the most members of legislature becomes the

   _____.

4. The leader of the party in power becomes the _____.

5. The premier is the leader of the _____ government.

6. The prime minister is the leader of the _____ government.

7. In Ontario, provincial elections generally happen every _____ years.

(B) Answer the Questions

1. Which party in Ontario's 2007 election had the most elected MPPs?

   _____

2. Which party became the party in power?

   _____

3. What is the website address for Elections Ontario?

   _____

4. How many politicians formed Ontario's legislature after the election of 2007?

   _____

5. When is the next election scheduled to happen in Ontario?

   _____

6. Who is the current premier of Ontario?

   _____

C Fill in the Blanks

Each province in Canada has its own provincial government led by a premier. The three territories have territorial governments.

Look through the newspaper. Try to find out the names of the premiers of each province and territory. Write the names of the premiers and the political party they belong to on the chart.

Province or Territory	Premier	Party in Power
British Columbia		
Alberta		
Saskatchewan		
Manitoba		
Ontario		
Quebec		
New Brunswick		
Nova Scotia		
Prince Edward Island		
Newfoundland and Labrador		
Yukon Territory		
Northwest Territories		
Nunavut		

Who is the premier of your province? _____

THE PROVINCIAL GOVERNMENT: THE CABINET

The premier is the leader of the provincial government. The premier chooses some members of the legislature to give him or her advice and help to form government policies. The members of legislature whom the premier chooses become cabinet ministers.

What Do Cabinet Ministers Do?

Each cabinet minister advises the premier on a provincial ministry. A ministry is a part of the government. The Ministry of Finance, Ministry of Education and Ministry of Social Services are examples of three ministries.

What Is the Cabinet?

The premier and the cabinet ministers are called the **Cabinet**.

What Does the Cabinet Do?

The Cabinet discusses how to spend government money and forms policies and ideas for new laws for the province. When members of the Cabinet agree on an idea for a new law, they write it down. It is called a bill.

The Cabinet presents the bill to the rest of the members of the provincial legislature. The legislature listens to the bill and discusses it. Then they vote on the bill. If most of the members of the legislature vote for the bill, the Lieutenant Governor signs the bill. It becomes a law for the province. The Lieutenant Governor represents the Queen in the provinces.

This is Ontario's Cabinet in 2009. There are 107 MPPs in the Ontario government. There are 26 cabinet ministers.

The provincial government works almost like the federal government. But there is no Senate in the provincial government.

Understand What You Read

(A) Fill in the Blanks

Write the correct letter on the lines to match the words with their meanings

_____ Premier a) The cabinet ministers and the premier

_____ Cabinet b) A rule

_____ Cabinet minister c) Leader of the provincial government

_____ Law d) Describes a proposed new law

_____ Bill e) A member of the provincial legislature whom the premier chooses to be part of the Cabinet

(B) Circle the Correct Answer

1. The Cabinet is made up of
   a) the premier and the cabinet ministers.
   b) the members of the provincial legislature.

2. The Cabinet presents bills to
   a) the premier.
   b) the members of the provincial legislature.

3. The premier chooses some members of the legislature to become
   a) cabinet ministers.
   b) Lieutenant Governor[s].

4. Provincial governments do not have
   a) a premier.
   b) a Senate.
   c) a Cabinet.

5. A cabinet minister advises the premier
   a) about a ministry.
   b) about the Senate.

THE PROVINCIAL GOVERNMENT:
THE LIEUTENANT GOVERNOR

Who Is the Lieutenant Governor?

Queen Elizabeth II is Canada's Head of State. The Governor General represents the Queen in Canada's federal government. There is also someone who represents the Queen in Canada's provincial governments. This person is called the Lieutenant Governor. There are ten Lieutenant Governors in Canada. There is one in each province.

The person who represents the Queen in the territories is called the Commissioner. There is a Commissioner in each territory.

What Does the Lieutenant Governor Do?

The Lieutenant Governor signs bills after the members of the legislature have voted for them. This makes the bills into provincial laws.

The Lieutenant Governor introduces new governments after each election. He or she also travels all over the province. He or she visits places and non-profit organizations and meets with people.

Steven L. Point is British Columbia's Lieutenant Governor.

How Does a Bill Become a Law in a Province?

Usually, the Cabinet writes a bill.

Then the Cabinet presents the bill to the rest of the members of the legislature.

The members of the provincial legislature vote on the bill.

If most of the members of the legislature vote for the bill, the Lieutenant Governor signs it. The bill becomes a law.

Understand What You Read

A **Circle the Correct Answer**

1. The _____ signs federal bills..   a) Governor General
   b) Lieutenant Governor

2. The _____ signs provincial bills.   a) Commissioner
   b) Lieutenant Governor

3. When the lieutenant governor signs a bill,   a) it becomes a law.
   b) the premier votes for it.

4. There are ten _____ in Canada.   a) Commissioners
   b) Lieutenant Governor
   c) Governor Generals

5. Queen Elizabeth II is Canada's   a) leader.
   b) Head of State.

B **Order**

Number the sentences in the correct order.

How a bill becomes a law in a province.

_____ The Cabinet presents the bill to the members of the provincial legislature.

_____ The Lieutenant Governor signs the bill to make it into a law.

_____ The Cabinet writes a bill.

_____ The members of the provincial legislature vote on the bill.

Who is the Lieutenant Governor for your province?

_____

THE PROVINCIAL GOVERNMENT: SUMMARY

Write the missing information in the box below.

You can call your provincial elections office. The number will be in the blue pages of the telephone book.

Provincial Government
Elections office phone number:
Lieutenant Governor:
Party in power:
Premier:
Year of last election:
My provincial riding:
My member of legislature:
Office address:
Office phone number:
E-mail address:

1. What is a member of the provincial legislature called in your province or territory?

    a) an MLA
    b) an MPP
    c) an MHA
    d) an MNA

2. What is the name of the government building in your province?

3. What city is it in?

THE PROVINCIAL AND FEDERAL GOVERNMENT: SUMMARY

Write the missing information on the chart below.

Provincial Government	Federal Government

Shade your province on the map.

Lieutenant Governor	_____	Governor General	_____
Party in power	_____	Party in power	_____
Premier	_____	Prime Minister	_____
Last election	_____	Last election	_____
My provincial riding	_____	My federal riding	_____
My MPP/MLA/MNA or MHA	_____	My MP	_____
Address	_____	My MP's address	_____
Phone number	_____	My MP's phone number	_____
E-mail address:	_____	My MP's e-mail address:	_____

THE MUNICIPAL GOVERNMENT

The municipal government is the government of a city, town, township or village. Another name for municipal government is local government. A municipality is a city, town, township or village.

There are hundreds of municipalities in Canada. In Ontario alone, there are about 475 municipalities.

What Does the Municipal Government Do?

Members of the municipal government make decisions for the people in the municipality. They decide how to spend municipal government money. They also make bylaws. A bylaw is a municipal law.

The municipal government makes decisions and bylaws about things like police, fire protection, jails, roads, hospitals, water and schools.

Do We Elect Members of the Municipal Government?

The people who live in each municipality elect members of the municipal government during municipal elections. Most municipalities have an election every three years.

Most municipalities are divided into voting areas called **wards**. Each ward has about the same number of people in it. The people in each ward elect one or two members of the municipal government to represent them. These elected members form the municipal government. They have meetings in the municipal government building, usually called City Hall.

Understand What You Read

A) Fill in the Blanks

List six things you think the municipal government makes decisions about.

1. _____   3. _____   5. _____

2. _____   4. _____   6. _____

B) Answer the Questions

1. What is another name for municipal government?

   _____

2. Who elects members of a municipal government?

   _____

3. What is a municipal law called?

   _____

4. Where does the municipal government have its meetings?

   _____

5. What are the voting areas called in a municipality?

   _____

THE MUNICIPAL GOVERNMENT: RESPONSIBILITIES

Where Does the Municipal Government Get Its Money?

The municipal government gets its money from many sources. The largest amount of money comes from property taxes.

The municipal government collects property taxes from people who own homes or businesses in the municipality.

The provincial and federal governments also give municipal governments some money every year. Municipal governments also get money from parking fines and other sources.

How Do Municipal Governments Spend Their Money?

Municipal governments spend their money on many things. Some of the things they spend money on are the following:

- Police
- Fire protection
- Public transportation
- Social services
- Water and sewage
- Libraries
- Parks
- Ambulance
- Airports
- Garbage and recycling
- Sidewalks
- Social housing

Each year, the municipal government announces a budget. The municipal budget is a plan that tells us how much money the government will spend on each area.

Understand What You Read

(A) **Answer the Questions**

1. List four sources of municipal government money.

   _____

2. Where does the municipal government get its largest amount of money?

   _____

3. Who pays property taxes?

   _____

4. List four things the government spends money on.

   _____

(B) **Match**

Write the correct letter on the lines to match each word with its meaning.

_____ Property   a) A city, town, township or village

_____ Property tax   b) A plan about how to save and spend money

_____ Municipality   c) Waste from toilets

_____ Sewage   d) Land

_____ Budget   e) Reuse

_____ Recycle   f) Tax you pay to the city for the property you own

(C) **Discuss**

1. Are you interested in municipal politics? Why or why not?

2. Many people write to the municipal government member who represents their ward. Sometimes they have a complaint. Sometimes they ask for something to make their neighbourhood safer, such as a traffic light on a busy road or extra lighting in a park.

   What do you think would make your neighbourhood safer or more enjoyable? Write a letter about it. You can send the letter to the municipal government member from your ward.

THE MUNICIPAL GOVERNMENT: MEMBERS OF GOVERNMENT

What Are the Members of Municipal Government Called?

Municipal governments work a little differently in different cities.

In most cities, the municipal government is called the Council, or the City Council. The people from each ward elect a member of Council. A member of Council is called a **councillor**. In some cities and towns, a councillor is called an **alderman** or **alderwoman**.

The Mayor

The people in the municipality also elect a leader of Council. The leader is called a **mayor**. In some municipalities, the leader is called a **reeve**.

Most municipalities also elect school board trustees. School board trustees make decisions about local schools.

Understand What You Read

(A) Fill in the Blanks

Try to fill in the blanks below.

Municipal Government	
Your municipality:	
Date of last election:	
Mayor:	
Name of your ward:	
Councillor for your ward:	
Your councillor's office address:	
Number of councillors in council:	
City Hall address:	
E-mail address:	

B Answer the Questions

alderman/alderwoman • wards • three • City Hall • mayor
bylaws • council • councillors • trustees • reeve

1. The leader of the municipal government is the _____.

2. Members of the municipal government are called _____.

3. In some municipalities, the mayor is called a _____.

4. In some municipalities, councillors are called _____.

5. The municipal government makes _____.

6. Every municipality is divided into voting areas called _____.

7. Municipal elections are usually every _____ years.

8. School board _____ make decisions about schools in the municipality.

9. The mayor and the councillors are the _____.

10. Council members have meetings in _____.

C Discuss

1. If you were a member of city council in your municipality, what changes would you make to bylaws about:

   • Parking
   • Parks
   • Smoking in restaurants
   • Public transportation
   • Garbage collection
   • Recycling

THE FEDERAL, PROVINCIAL AND MUNICIPAL GOVERNMENT: REVIEW

Understand What You Read

A Sort

Each of the words below relates to either the federal, provincial or municipal government.

Write the words under the correct headings in the chart. The first word is done for you.

☑ Premier   ☐ City Hall   ☐ MLA

☐ Senators   ☐ Senate   ☐ Bylaw

☐ Laws   ☐ Councillor   ☐ Prime minister

☐ Laws   ☐ Mayor   ☐ Alderman/alderwoman

☐ Ward   ☐ MPP   ☐ Riding

☐ Cabinet   ☐ One   ☐ Riding

☐ Cabinet   ☐ Member of Parliament   ☐ Ten

☐ Lieutenant Governor   ☐ Member of the Legislative Assembly   ☐ Municipality

☐ MP   ☐ Governor General   ☐ Hundreds

☐ Member of Provincial Parliament   ☐ Reeve   ☐ Council

Federal Government	Provincial Government	Municipal Government
	premier	

B Wordsearch

The words in the word list are hidden in the wordsearch puzzle in the box below. The words go across →, down ↓, and diagonally ↘. Find and circle the words. The first one is circled for you.

```
C F E B G O V E R N O R G E N E R A L N D T J
A A E L E C T I O N P O C I P M E M L A E P S
R G M D S L I B E R A L F A D A E F M P M R S
C C P P E D C P R E M I E R N A V V M P O I E
W A R D A R F L W E U I F Y M D E M P P C M D
S B B I L L A I S E N A T O R E I L B I R E A
E E I I B P G L A W I V O T E S E D E N A M T
P B N N N N N V H C M R R C B Y B A C C I M
T K A A E P R O V I N C I A L Y A F T Y N A
L O L O T T T D T Y P R D D N D P L B E E I Y
E O J G E E D C A N A D A I P N D L A E B S O
C V W E H I R A D U L T S N A E D O L W I T R
C O U N C I L L O R Y Q F G I S G T L E L E T
H O U S E O F C O M M O N S G H A W O Y L R E
G P A R T Y I N P O W E R P O L I T I C I A N
```

Word List

☑ Adult   ☐ Federal   ☐ Party in power
☐ Ballot   ☐ Governor General   ☐ Politician
☐ Bill   ☐ House of Commons   ☐ Premier
☐ Bylaw   ☐ Law   ☐ Prime Minister
☐ Cabinet   ☐ Liberal   ☐ Provincial
☐ Campaign   ☐ Mayor   ☐ Reeve
☐ Canada   ☐ MLA   ☐ Riding
☐ Candidate   ☐ MP   ☐ Senate
☐ Councillor   ☐ MPP   ☐ Senator
☐ Democracy   ☐ Municipal   ☐ Vote
☐ Election   ☐ NDP   ☐ Ward

C Complete the Crossword

The crossword clues and word list are on the next page.

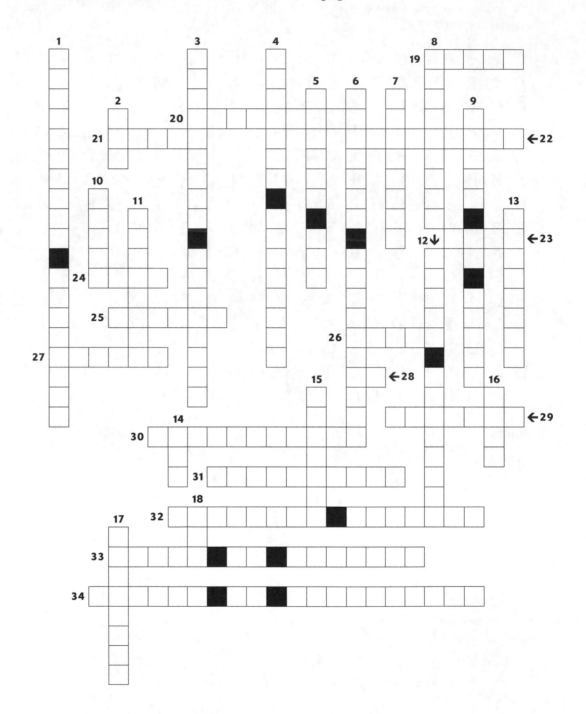

Use the clues below to complete the crossword on the previous page.

If the crossword is too difficult, use the word list at the bottom of the page.

DOWN ↓

1. Represents the Queen in the provinces
2. A rule Canadians must obey
3. Another word for a riding
4. A member of the Cabinet
5. A box we put our ballots into after we vote
6. Government of Canada
7. The month before voting day
8. City government is ____ government.
9. The party with the most elected MPs
10. A municipal law
11. Number of provincial and territorial governments
12. The leader of the federal government
13. When we vote for new members of government
14. Short for New Democratic Party
15. The leader of the provincial government
16. To put a mark on a ballot
17. Last name of the prime minister in 2002
18. The number of federal governments in Canada

ACROSS →

19. The leader of the municipal government
20. A person who enters an election campaign
21. A person who is 18 or older
22. When the people govern themselves
23. Describes a new law
24. A municipal voting area
25. A part of the Parliament of Canada
26. Another name for mayor, in some cities
27. A voting area
28. Short for member of parliament
29. A member of the Senate
30. A candidate who doesn't belong to a party
31. A municipal politician
32. The Queen's representative in Canada
33. All the MPs are members of the ____ ____ ____.
34. MP stands for ____ ____ ____.

Word List

Governor General • cabinet minister • premier • reeve • election
Mayor • law • independent • PM • municipal • candidate
Lieutenant Governor • democracy • campaign • Chrétien • one
ballot box • bylaw • ward • bill • prime minister
federal government • adult • riding • councillor • senator
vote • party in power • electoral district • thirteen • Senate
NDP • House of Commons • MP

Adult:	A person eighteen years old or older
Alderman or alderwoman:	A municipal politician, sometimes called a councillor
Ballot:	A piece of paper with the names of candidates for voting
Ballot box:	A box our ballots go into after we have voted
Bill:	Describes a new law
Bylaw:	A municipal law
Cabinet:	The federal Cabinet is the prime minister and cabinet ministers; the provincial Cabinet is the premier and cabinet ministers
Cabinet ministers:	Members of the legislature the prime minister or premier chooses to advise him or her on an area of government
Candidate:	A person who enters an election campaign to become a member of government
Commissioner:	The Queen's representative in the territories
Constituency:	A riding
Councillor:	A municipal politician
Democracy:	A system in which people govern themselves
Election:	A time we vote for new members of government
Election campaign:	A time candidates try to convince us to vote for them
Electoral district:	A riding
Federal government:	The government of Canada
Governor General:	The Queen's representative for the federal government
House of Commons:	All the Members of Parliament, or MPs
Independent:	A candidate or politician who does not belong to a political party
Law:	A rule Canadians must obey
Legislature:	The people who can make laws; usually refers to the people we elect in provincial or territorial elections
Lieutenant Governor:	The Queen's representative in the provinces
Mayor:	The leader of the municipal government
MHA:	Member of the House of Assembly; the name for members of the provincial legislature in Newfoundland and Labrador
Ministry:	An area or department of government
MLA:	Member of the Legislative Assembly; the name for members of the provincial legislature in most provinces
MNA:	Member of the National Assembly; the name for members of the provincial legislature in Quebec
MP:	Member of Parliament

MPP:	Member of Provincial Parliament; the name for members of the provincial legislature in Ontario
Municipal government:	Government of a city, town or community
Municipality:	A city, town or community
Parliament of Canada:	The Queen, the House of Commons and the Senate
Party in power:	The political party with the most elected members of government
Political party:	A group of people with similar ideas about how to govern Canada
Politician:	A member of government
Premier:	The leader of the provincial or territorial government
Prime minister:	The leader of the federal government
Provincial government:	The government of a province
Reeve:	The leader of the municipal government in some municipalities
Riding:	A voting area
Senate:	A part of the federal government
Senators:	Members of the Senate
Territorial government:	The government of a territory
Vote:	To put a mark on a ballot beside the name of a candidate
Voters' list:	A list of Canadians who can vote
Ward:	A municipal voting area

Aboriginal peoples:
A group of North American Indians who share the same customs

Adult:
A person eighteen years old or older

Alderman or alderwoman:
A municipal politician, sometimes called a Councillor

Ancestor:
A relative from a long time ago, like a great-grandparent

Atlantic region:
Nova Scotia, New Brunswick, Prince Edward Island and Newfoundland and Labrador

Ballot:
A piece of paper with the names of candidates for voting

Ballot box:
A box our ballots go into after we have voted

Band:
The first people to live in a country

Bank of Canada:
A government bank that helps to keep Canada's economy healthy and also makes Canada's bills

Bilingual:
Having two languages

Bill:
Describes a new law

BNA Act:
The British North American Act; a law signed by the British government in 1867 that explained how Canada would govern itself

British North America:
The land in North America that belonged to Britain (from 1763 to 1867)

Bylaw:
A municipal law

Cabinet:
The federal Cabinet is the prime minister and cabinet ministers; the provincial Cabinet is the premier and cabinet ministers

Cabinet ministers:
Members of the legislature the prime minister or premier chooses to advise him or her on an area of government

Canada:
The northernmost country in North America

Canada Day:
A holiday on July 1 celebrating Canada's birthday

Canada Pension Plan:
A government pension for Canadians who have worked in Canada and have reached the age of 65

Canada's breadbasket:
Another name for the Prairie provinces

Canadian Shield:
A large area of rock in Canada

Candidate:
A person who enters an election campaign to become a member of the government

Capital city:
The city in which the government is based

Celsius:
A unit of metric measurement used to measure temperature

Census:
An official count of the population

Central Canada:
Ontario and Quebec

Charter of Rights and Freedoms:
Part of Canada's Constitution; lists basic rights of Canadians

Coal:
A black mineral burned to make electricity

Coast:
Land beside the ocean

Colony:
Land a country owns that is far away

Commissioner:
The Queen's representative in the territories

Confederation:
The union of different areas of land

Constituency:
A riding

Constitution Act:
The new name for the BNA Act in 1982

Continent:
A large area of land

Councillor:
A municipal politician

Currency:
Types of bills and coins that make up a money system

Deductions:
Amounts of money subtracted from income

Democracy:
A system in which people govern themselves

East Coast:
Another name for the Atlantic region

Election:
A time we vote for new members of the government

Election campaign:
A time candidates try to convince us to vote for them

Electoral district:
A riding

Employment Insurance:
A government program that helps people who lose their job (when it is not their fault)

Eskimo:
Another name for the Inuit

Federal government:
The government of Canada

First Nations:
Another name for the North American Indians

Fur trade:
The trade in beaver furs between Aboriginal peoples and Europeans

Governor General:
The Queen's representative for the federal government

Great Lakes:
Five large lakes in southern Ontario

Gross pay:
Income before deductions

House of Commons:
All the Members of Parliament, or MPs

Hudson Bay:
A large body of water in the middle of Canada

Humid:
Moist

Hydroelectricity:
Electricity made from moving water

Immigrant:
Someone who was born in one country, then moved to another country to live

Independent (country):
Self-governing

Independent (politician):
A candidate or politician who does not belong to a political party

Inuit:
A group of Aboriginal people who live in the North of Canada

Inuktitut:
The language of the Inuit

Kanata:
A word that means village in an Aboriginal language

Law:
A rule Canadians must obey

Legislature:
The people who can make laws; usually refers to the people we elect in provincial or territorial elections

Lieutenant Governor:
The Queen's representative in the provinces

Loyalists:
People who moved from the United States to Canada after the United States became independent

Manufacturing industry:
Includes jobs that produce the things we buy and use every day

Mayor:
The leader of the municipal government

Métis:
People descended from North American Indians and Europeans

Metric system:
A system for measuring distance, weight, mass and temperature

MHA:
Member of the House of Assembly; the name for members of the provincial legislature in Newfoundland and Labrador

Minimum wage:
The lowest hourly wage an employer can pay you

Ministry:
An area or department of government

MLA:
Member of the Legislative Assembly; the name for members of the provincial legislature in most provinces

MNA:
Member of the National Assembly; the name for members of the provincial legislature in Quebec

Mother tongue:
The first language a person learns and still understands

Mount Logan:
Canada's highest mountain

MP:
Member of Parliament

MPP:
Member of Provincial Parliament; the name for members of the provincial legislature in Ontario

Municipal government:
Government of a city, town or community

Municipality:
A city, town or community

National Aboriginal Day:
On June 21; celebrates Aboriginal peoples

Natural resource:
Something found in nature that can be used, like water, forests, minerals or fish

Natural resource industry:
Includes jobs that extract natural resources from the land

Net pay:
Income after deductions

New France:
French colonies in what is now Canada

North (the):
Yukon Territory, the Northwest Territories and Nunavut

North America:
A continent that includes Canada, the United States and Mexico

North American Indians:
A group of Aboriginal peoples

Official language:
The language the government uses

Parliament Buildings:
The federal government buildings in Ottawa

Parliament of Canada:
The Queen, the House of Commons and the Senate

Party in power:
The political party with the most elected members of government

Pension:
Money paid regularly to a person, usually after he or she turns 65

Political party:
A group of people with similar ideas about how to govern Canada

Politician:
A member of government

Population:
The number of people living in a country or area

Prairie provinces:
Manitoba, Saskatchewan and Alberta

Premier:
The leader of the provincial or territorial government

Prime minister:
The leader of the federal government

Property tax:
A yearly tax we pay for living on property

Provincial government:
The government of a province

Reeve:
The leader of the municipal government in some municipalities

Reserves:
Areas of land saved for North American Indians

Riding:
A voting area

Rocky Mountains:
Mountains in Western Canada

Royal Canadian Mint:
Makes Canada's coins

Sales tax:
A tax on products and services we buy

Sedimentary rock:
Rock made by rivers carrying sediment

Senate:
A part of the federal government

Senators:
Members of the Senate

Service industry:
Includes jobs that serve people with the things they want

Settlers:
People who move to a new undeveloped land to live

Statistics Canada:
Offers information about the results of the census

Taxes:
Amounts of money (on income, property and products) that go to the government

Temperate:
Not too hot and not too cold

Territorial government:
The government of a territory

The thirteen colonies:
British colonies in parts of what is now the United States

Trans-Canada Highway:
A highway that crosses southern Canada

Unemployment rate:
The number of unemployed people for every 100 adults who are looking for work

Vancouver Island:
An island of British Columbia

Victoria Day:
A holiday in May that celebrates Queen Victoria's birthday

Vote:
To put a mark on a ballot beside the name of a candidate

Voters' list:
A list of Canadians who can vote

Ward:
A municipal voting area

Wheat:
A grain used to make bread